Construction

Leadership

Success

The Construction Foreman's Definitive
Guide for Running Safe, Efficient,
and Profitable Projects

Construction

Leadership

Success

JASON C. McCARTY

Acknowledgments

I want to begin by thanking my loving wife Carrie. Without your encouragement, support, and patience this book would most certainly have remained on my list of "things to do."

To my family, thank you for your support. I am proud to say that I come from a long line of individuals who have always been willing to put in a hard day's work.

I am convinced that if it weren't for the willingness of the following individuals to share their knowledge and offer their guidance, my career may have taken a less fulfilling path: Bob Halliday, Kent Mofford, Wade Terry, Dale Woodward, Craig Davis, Rich Hardy, and Bob Grovom. Although there are many people along the way who have contributed to my base of skill and knowledge, I hold these craftsmen in the highest regard.

To the overseas group (you all know who you are), I consider being a part of your expert team a privilege.

Throughout the process of writing this book there have been a few friends/coworkers who have been sounding boards for my ideas, philosophies, and, on occasion, frustration-fueled rants. I now realize that I never asked any of you if you were interested in being willing participants, so thank you for never telling me to get lost. I refer to this group as "X5": Shawn Marlatt, "Freaky" Johnson, Seth McCready, James Stewart, and Geoff DaVault.

Finally, I want to thank my editor, Heidi Connolly. Your expertise, professionalism, and obvious passion for your work has made every part of this process an enlightening and enjoyable experience.

Table of Contents

Part Two: Planning — 73

Part Three: Organization — 137

Part Four: People Skills   169

Part Five: Stress Management   265

Note from Author

Because it has been my own reading experience that use of both male and female pronouns tends to be a distraction that can hinder thorough comprehension, whereas use of a single pronoun can allow for a more rhythmic reading experience and make it easier to focus on the subject matter, I have chosen to use the male pronoun exclusively in this book.

These examples should demonstrate my point:

1. "When a foreman is putting his or her plan together he/she should always consider the installations of every other trade in addition to his/her own." (This approach is disruptive.)

2. "When a foreman is putting their plan together they should always consider the installations of every other trade in addition to their own." (This is grammatically incorrect.)

3. "When a foreman is putting his plan together he should always consider the installations of every other trade in addition to his own." (This works; it's simple and effective.)

In no way is my decision meant to be a slight to the countless skilled women employed in the construction trades or to their contribution to the industry. The many lessons I've learned and conclusions I've reached have been formed over 20 years working side by side with men and women alike.

–Jason McCarty, 2011

Preface

Construction Leadership Success is designed to be a useful guide for any construction industry foreman who is searching for industry specific advice in both leadership and project management techniques.

As a skilled trades person makes the transition from working as a journeyman to becoming a well-rounded and effective foreman, there is an enormous shift in thinking that needs to occur. For some, the transformation comes easily, while others spend their entire career in search of success. It is my belief that the ability to adapt is largely based on two things: work experience and a thorough understanding of the new responsibilities that go along with becoming a foreman for the first time. When either of these things are missing, or missing in enough quantity, success becomes much less of a certainty.

Whether you are working towards becoming a foreman, are a first-time foreman, or have been running work for years, this book can help you. Following my suggestions will help you raise your awareness, elevate your abilities, and gain a broad understanding of what it takes to be a successful foreman in the construction industry.

The information, suggestions, and opinions contained here apply to every construction trade and have been gained through my real-world experiences over the last 20 years, during which time I have worked as a material handler, apprentice, journeyman, and foreman on numerous commercial and industrial construction projects.

My objective when I began this endeavor was to put together a book that contained valuable knowledge and useful advice that would give readers a baseline level of understanding that they would otherwise be left to learn over many years of trial and error. I truly believe that if you are a skilled trades person and are willing to follow the recommendations given in this book, it will only be a matter of time before you will earn the reputation of being a great leader.

In order for you to fully understand some of the ideas I have about this subject, and for you to support those ideas as credible in their conclusions, I believe it will benefit you to know a little about my background. Although many of the challenges you will face may not fall directly in line with my own experiences, many of the lessons I have learned still hold an educational value spanning the many layers of the construction contracting business.

Let me say right up front that I do not claim to be a psychologist. Nor do I hold a degree in business. What I do possess that a degree in psychology or business cannot provide is two decades of insight and experience that evolved one day at a time. Like most folks who become foremen, I started at the very bottom of our industry and slowly moved my way up the ladder through hard work and determination. My entire work life has been spent in the field, working with the tools, managing crews, or running entire projects. Unlike the many authors of other leadership and management books, who are well versed in office management and corporate leadership techniques, my leadership knowledge and suggestions are based solely on the unique challenges that a construction foreman faces on a daily basis.

Furthermore, in my many years in this business I have seen it from all angles, from the perspective of a teenager delivering material and tools to job sites, to an adult involved in managing many projects, both large and small, from beginning to end. It is because of my experiences, both good and bad, along with my curiosity about the different strategies and techniques foremen use to run projects, that I have been motivated to observe and then contemplate what works, what doesn't, and why. What has probably been the most surprising result is that I have come to realize that most foremen (including myself) never receive any formal training in planning, organization, people skills, leadership, or management. The outcome of this critical omission is that many projects are run with the absence of a well-thought-out plan or strategy, leaving little or no hope that a project will reach its maximum potential for profitability.

When I was offered my first foreman position, I immediately looked for a book that could help me define and understand my new responsibilities. It wasn't out there. That's why this book is created to be a road map to success, one that will get you there sooner than later and will steer you around some of those same bumps in the road that I didn't know how to avoid.

Looking back, I believe my curiosity about planning and production started early in my career as an apprentice electrician. I noticed things that I thought the foreman could be doing to help his crew and to help the project in general be more efficient and productive. The truth is I had no idea what the full responsibilities of the foreman were so I was in no position to judge his abilities. Of course at the time I was also unconscious (in the way of most youth) of that fact, so I continually questioned in my mind why some projects went smoothly and others appeared to flounder or end up in total disarray. What became abundantly clear, even back then, was that a foreman who was organized and had a well-ordered plan always made finishing projects on time and within budget look easy. Meanwhile, the foremen for whom I worked who had a "shoot from the hip" mentality and who always appeared to be in a constant state of panic tended to scramble almost aimlessly through their projects from start to finish.

Shortly after finishing a five-year apprenticeship and becoming a licensed electrician, I was offered a foreman position. I wasn't sure if I had what it would take to be a foreman, but I decided that if my company was offering me the opportunity, I'd better take it. You may be surprised, therefore, to hear me say that although I learned valuable lessons as a result, I feel this was an error in judgment, and one that turned out to be a huge mistake. In the next few pages it should become apparent why.

I hope that after you read about some of my early trials and tribulations and about some of the hard lessons I learned along the way, you'll be in a much stronger position for finding your own place in the construction industry and your own success as a construction foreman. (Jason C. McCarty, 2011)

Introduction

I was 16 years old in the summer of 1987. I was sitting on the couch on the first day of my summer break from school when my dad asked me what I was planning on doing for the next three months. My response was probably pretty typical. I told him I was trying to figure it out, but really I assumed it meant hanging out with friends... going down to the river...generally having a good time. I had plenty of ideas, but none of them even remotely suggested I was thinking seriously about work or being especially productive.

My dad was working for an electrical contractor as an electrician turned project manager at the time. He told me his company needed someone to come to the shop and wash some of their trucks for a few days. Would I be interested in making some extra money? I had a part-time job working at a burger joint, a job I wasn't exactly thrilled about, so when he offered me double what they were paying I jumped on it. Little did I know that snap decision would profoundly change the direction of my life.

When I showed up at the shop on my first day I didn't know anything about anything, and I'd only had my driver's license for about three months. I was the typical teenage kid who didn't have a clue about the real world and how things worked.

THE REAL WORLD

I hadn't been washing trucks for long before they had me out making material deliveries to job sites all over town. I probably learned more during that summer than I had in my entire life up to that point. I learned everything from reading a road map to how to properly tie down the material in the back of a pickup truck.

This particular lesson stemmed from the time that I pulled out into the street with a load of conduit in the back of my truck only to have it spill out onto the road and almost hit the luxury car of the owner of the company as he pulled into work. Let me tell you, I sprang out of that truck so fast the pipe didn't have time to hit the road. Then I loaded it all back into the truck lightning quick and headed off to make the delivery, all without looking up to see how much of an impression my driving and I had made on the boss. I did make sure to drive extra slowly around corners after that. *(Real World Lesson #1: Note to self—Slow down around corners.)*

When I returned to the shop after my deliveries, I was not surprised to be called into my dad's office, where the owner and he had been meeting to discuss business and the "new driver." I didn't have any trouble imagining the look on my dad's face when the owner had asked him, "Who's the new driver, and where did you find that genius?" I know it was more than a little painful for Dad to admit that it had been his son in the truck. Needless to say, I got a good ass-chewing. And that's when I learned my second of many lessons about the real world and the construction industry. *(Real World Lesson #2: Note to self—Tie things down.)*

After I finished getting an earful from my Dad about how I should have known enough to have the pipe tied down, I simply responded that it wasn't my fault because no one had told me to tie it down. Evidently that was the wrong thing to say. I'll spare you the gory details of what happened next, but I'm sure you can figure out that the conversation was not over at that point. *(Real World Lessons 3, 4, 5, and 6: Note to self—Don't try to talk your way out of taking responsibility for your actions).*

I will not bore you with every other single tough lesson I ever learned in the last 20 years either, but I hope you'll take away the fact that I wasn't always a quick study and that I needed to take full advantage of the lessons as they were bestowed on me in order to not repeat the same mistakes over and over.

GROWING UP

By the time the next summer rolled around my Dad had left that company to start his own electrical contracting business. I continued working for him that season delivering materials and tools and doing odds and ends around the shop.

After graduating from high school the next year and a little time had passed, my Dad asked me one day if I was interested in applying for the five-year electrical apprenticeship to become a licensed journeyman electrician. I had thought about it some, but at the time I wasn't sure if it was the right path for me. After some consideration, though, when the next opportunity came around to apply I decided I'd go for it, and was very fortunate to be accepted into the program on my first attempt.

I was on my way.

While I was completing my apprenticeship I worked for a large company that employed some very talented craftsmen with whom I felt privileged to work. In fact, I still work with many of these same individuals to this day. Back then, not only were they knowledgeable about the trade, but always willing to teach me everything they knew—tricks of the trade, how to work hard without hurting myself, and good practices for working safely and efficiently. The skills I learned from these craftsmen during my five years in training to become a journeyman electrician have proved to be invaluable to me throughout my career.

PROMOTED

About a month after I received my electrical license I got a call from one of the managers at my company who said he wanted to talk to me about an opportunity. During that meeting he offered me a foreman position on a project that would be a year long and built from the ground up, a brand new elementary school. I have to admit that I was both excited and overwhelmed at the same time. Due to my inexperience, I was not only unable to clearly gauge how difficult the project would be, but I had no way of anticipating the long-term lasting effects it would have on me.

As soon as I was on site it was as if I'd been shot out of a cannon. I didn't know how to plan properly. I didn't know how to prioritize what needed to be done. Soon I found myself inundated by all the responsibilities that were now mine because I was the foreman. I had been put in a position and was expected to perform, but I had no basis for understanding and had not been told anything about what my new job would entail. No one ever said, "Hey, what do you know about running a job? How do you feel about it? Do you need some help?" It felt just like it had when I hadn't known enough to tie down the pipe in the truck and no one had thought to mention a thing.

The assumption was "Hey, Jason's a hard worker; he's always been reliable and trustworthy. He'll probably make a good foreman." Again, as flattering as it was to be asked, I wasn't even close to being ready.

As the project progressed, I continued to struggle to competently understand, let alone manage, all my new responsibilities. Since one thing I'd never learned throughout my apprenticeship was how a foreman needs to build a comprehensive job-specific plan, it should come as no surprise that I fell behind early. I was playing catch-up from day one. I became that foreman I talked about earlier—the one who shoots from the hip and remains in a constant state of panic. I solved some problems by throwing more manpower at them and others by flying by the seat of my pants, all while trying to make the best decisions possible. You might say it was a very stressful time.

Unfortunately, the further along the job continued, the harder it was to manage. By the time the job was finished a year later, I was working twelve hours a day and wasn't sleeping very well at night. That project had become my whole life, leaving me very little time for anything else. I am proud to say that I finished the project, but it definitely took a toll on me both mentally and physically.

Once the project was completed and it was time to tally up the damage, the net loss for my company was $250,000. It was a huge blow to my confidence. I had spent five years working for people who wanted me around and who told me I was doing a good job. But now I felt like a complete failure. It was not a good way to start out my career as a foreman.

The good news is that I was very fortunate that the management team at my company who had known me for all those years I was an apprentice was confident I had done my best. In fact, believe it or not, they asked me to run another project. Who knows? Maybe they figured they had just paid for some of the most expensive on-the-job training ever recorded and that it was in their best interest to try and get a return on their investment. So, as beat down as I was, I was also determined to prove I could be successful, and I decided that having a better understanding of how to approach my responsibilities was the answer.

RUNNING WORK

Since those early days of struggling to learn the ropes I have continued to run work, and when I am not working as a foreman I work as a journeyman for other foremen in my company.

It has come to my attention over the years since that first disaster (my *attempt* at running work) that this kind of experience is the typical trial-by-fire education foremen are likely to get, and a common practice in every construction trade. When someone new is promoted to the position of foreman, he is mostly left to figure out how to be successful on his own. In fact, I often wonder how much money continues to be squandered by contractors who choose to ignore their foremen's lack of knowledge in basic business comprehension, planning, leadership skills, and managing and motivating others.

Once I realized mine was not an isolated case, I asked myself why. Why was there such a shortage of training available for a new foreman? Why was there no training at all for those who wished to enhance the abilities they already had when it was so clear that it was so badly needed? As I worked around more and more foremen and watched how they worked, it became all too clear that the flaws in their approaches existed not because they weren't trying, but because they'd never been taught to do things differently. This meant that the mistakes they were making they had been making since day one.

What I also found is that if you learn to do something the wrong way but continue to experience enough success to get by, there is rarely any motivation to want to change yourself or what you're doing. I have worked with many individuals, including coworkers, who fall into this category. Thrown into the fire early on, they do whatever they have to do in order to get the job done, and as long as they manage to do their job or make a small profit for the company they continue to run work. It's a vicious cycle—and a lot of money gets wasted in the process.

AIMING HIGH

There are some people who are all right with doing the minimum as long as they can keep their job and make a decent living. I do not happen to be one of them. I believe when you take a foreman position, you should treat your responsibilities as if your own money is on the line. It may be that I see things a little differently because I have watched my dad run his own contracting business and have seen the sacrifices he had to make and the amount of financial risk owning a business can create. I have always been well aware of the far-reaching consequences that a less than inspired attempt on a foreman's part can produce. That's why if you are inspired to aim high and never settle for average or minimal results once you've read this book, I will have done the job I set out to do.

But before you head down the path of being a foreman, I want you to consider this. There is a very simple, normally unspoken and unwritten contract that exists between a foreman and his company. If this contract were to be put into text it might read, "The company agrees to provide a steady source of income, plus possible future opportunities, in exchange for the foreman doing everything within his power to complete projects on time and, ideally, under budget." If every foreman accepted and acknowledged this unwritten agreement in full, I believe he would never stop searching for ways to improve his abilities.

❏

Construction Leadership Success is broken down into five key parts based on the skills every successful foreman needs for use on the job:

I.   Contracting business basics

II. Planning

III. Organization

IV. People skills

V.   Stress management

Each skill category covers the vital things you need to know to become a successful foreman in the construction industry. As you read this book, consider how the advice applies to your specific trade and its unique challenges. I encourage you to take notes, highlight important information, and mark pages for future reference. You can never be sure what the future holds; at some point in your career you may find it helpful to revisit some, if not all, of these topics.

IT'S A PROCESS

Becoming a successful foreman is a process. Be dedicated to that process and be prepared to face some adversity. What will ultimately determine your level of success is how you cope with this adversity and how you approach and conquer daily challenges. In the end, commitment, determination, and work ethic are the forces that will carry you as far as you want to go in this business.

I hope those of you who read this book discover the answers you seek and find success, prosperity, and opportunity that leads you down the path to a long, happy, and rewarding career.

CONTRACTING

BUSINESS

BASICS

Chapter 1

The Mentality of a Contractor

DO YOU HAVE WHAT IT TAKES?

What does it take to be a great construction foreman? At the very least, it takes a basic understanding of the contracting business from top to bottom. That's why we're going to start by discussing what the business end of our profession looks like from the contractor's perspective.

As you read this book, consider the job responsibilities and the mind set that you'll be expected to have if and when you take a foreman position with your company. Many foremen make the mistake of looking at their responsibilities strictly based on what they need to accomplish each day to keep their projects moving forward. The difference between top-notch foremen and those who find themselves stuck on a lower rung of success is not just a matter of intelligence and skill, however. These tradesmen also have a firm understanding regarding the *business* of construction. This includes everything from the estimating process the contractor uses to bid on a project to financial considerations that can affect the contractor's ability to perform in a manner that allows him to stay in business.

A foreman who is educated in matters like these is always better equipped to identify potential problems before they occur. This knowledge also helps him make informed decisions as he plans and guides his crew through the building process.

It would be difficult for someone to truly understand the contracting business and how it works without first looking at the business from the company owner's point of view. The contracting business is a very competitive and pressure-filled industry, one where it is critical for contractors to distinguish themselves from their competitors. No matter what trade you are in or the services you provide, there is always another company who is willing to offer the same product and installation at a price that is close to, or less than, yours. Therefore, being successful in the contracting business means two things: providing excellent customer service and delivering quality work performed at a fair price.

THE CONTRACTOR'S DILEMMA

By virtue of the fact that every contractor needs to provide superior service and work, he will always face the same dilemma, that of competition. It is the bane of every company to be in direct competition with other local contractors who are competing for the same customers in a market area that will always be limited by geographical location. (I realize there are some contractors who work in more than one state and/or internationally, but for our purposes we'll focus on those cities where the majority of contractors who compete for projects are local.)

For the sake of argument, let's suppose that each contractor in our geographical area that bids on the same project is more than capable of supplying the customer with what he needs. Naturally, this places each company in the precarious position of continually searching for new ways to set itself apart from the competition. Some of these ways have a negative effect, like cutting corners during an installation, something that can cause the company to earn a bad reputation and lead to difficulty procuring future projects. Obviously, bidding projects at too high a price also has a negative outcome because the company probably won't be selected for the job. On the other hand, winning a bid as the low bidder is too easy; anyone can do take-offs on a project, tally up the labor and material costs, and then slash the quote below the competition. The only real way to run a successful contracting business is to find a way to do it for less, and do it while still providing a first-rate product.

This is where the foreman comes in. The contractor relies heavily on every foreman and the teams he leads to complete the company's projects on time. The contractor is well aware that to do that, and do it under budget, the project will have to be run efficiently and productively in every way.

The ironic thing about being an owner/contractor is that most individuals in this position have decided to become owners based on their own knowledge and abilities, including how they approach running projects and how they take care of their customers' needs. But now that they are running the company their role as the hands-on leader during the actual construction of a project disappears. Now most of their involvement with the project and the customer is around the process of estimating and bidding. This is the time when they (the owners), along with their estimators and management team, make promises and commitments to the customer that they hope and pray will later be carried out by the foremen and their teams. The contractor knows that the life of the project is in the hands of these foremen on every single project. The contractor must be able to rely on his foremen to take care of the customer in the manner he has been promised and to be a good representative of their company.

Ultimately, the contractor knows that having the right foremen means having foremen who clearly understand the vision the contractor has for his company and the services it provides.

Knowing that this dilemma faces all contractors, you may wonder why anyone would take the risk. But there are always people who believe they have what it takes and are willing to take whatever risks exist to achieve their goals.

TAKING THE RISK TO GO IT ALONE

If you believe you have what it takes to run a contracting business, you're probably up for both the challenges and potential rewards such an undertaking encompasses. For many who feel they have reached a plateau in their career as a foreman or project manager, the challenges of setting out on one's own is too tempting to disregard. For these individuals who possess the drive and desire, it's worth the risk in order to be able to do things their way.

Sometimes a group of individuals comes together to start a contracting business. One common explanation for this kind of partnership is that the individuals involved believe that together their combined experience and strengths will create a successful company. Another obvious reason is that no one individual will be taking on all the financial risk because the group will share in the financial obligations created by the new venture. To sum it up, a group generally has benefits the individual does not: the luxury of collective experience, skills, and financial resources.

Although the examples above address some of the ancillary reasons for starting a contracting business, we all know that financial success is what really drives certain individuals to take on the added risk. If it weren't for the desire for financial improvement most would not bother subjecting themselves to the stress and pressures that are habitually linked to owning a contracting business.

THE LIFE OF A CONTRACTOR

If you've never really thought about the process your contractor has to undergo in order to procure a project for you to run, now's the time. Most of us can't possibly appreciate what an involved, painstaking process it is either, one full of ups and downs and plenty of uncertainty. I'll do my best to give you a simple example of how it works here.

First of all, your contractor has to learn about the project, perhaps by word of mouth, a bid registry, or by a customer's invitation. Once the contractor decides to bid on the project, he will access a set of complete blueprints/specifications from which he and his team will begin to envision the project—to build it from start to finish—in their minds. This is where experienced estimators and project managers earn their money. During the estimating process it is crucial that nothing gets missed and every aspect of the installation is taken into consideration. It is a delicate balance between recognizing the elements that are known factors and making educated guesses about all the other unknown factors. The fact is that no one can know for sure if the project has been bid correctly until midway through or even later in the building process. If the contractor bids the project too high he won't get the job; too low and he may end up in a losing situation before the project ever gets started.

When a contractor is lucky enough to be awarded a project as the low bidder, everyone involved from managers to estimators is ecstatic because all their hard work has paid off. They'd spent weeks, even months, doing take-offs and calculations and sending out equipment and material lists to get quotes. Then they sharpened their pencils to make sure the right number was put at the top. Now it's paid off and they are on top of the world.

For the moment.

Shortly after the euphoria of getting the project wears off, usually anywhere from ten minutes to a few hours after hearing the news, an overwhelming feeling of doubt inevitably starts to creep in. *Why were we low? Did we leave something out? I wonder how low we actually were? Who are we going to get to be our foremen?* These are some of the questions that race through the minds of the contracting team as the initial high quickly starts to fade away. It may be contrary to what you might think, but once the bloom is off the rose, I'd be willing to bet that most contractors don't sleep very well the night after they've been awarded a big project due to all the worrying that sets in.

CHOOSING THE FOREMAN

The other crucial moment that will determine the success of this project is the moment the foreman is chosen. Whoever the contractor chooses to run the new project has to be able to manage an efficient and productive job site every step of the way. This foreman is the only person who will be on the front lines, making daily—and minute to minute—decisions that will ultimately determine the outcome of the job. Sure, this foreman will still have support from the company's estimators and the project manager involved in the bidding process, but the truth is that once the project starts those people will no longer be significant contributors because they will be off searching for and then estimating future projects for the company. It makes sense that compared to the foreman these individuals will have little time and involvement in the project as it moves forward.

On-the-job Training: Thinking Like a Contractor

Consider all that you've read up to this point. Take a minute now and ask yourself if you have what it takes to risk everything you own to create a contracting business where you will have to count on someone else to protect your company's best interests. Imagine how it will feel when you can't watch over the shoulder of that person because he is in a location that isn't always easily accessible. Imagine how it will feel when even if you can access the location easily and regularly, you don't have time because your job as the owner is to make sure your company has the money and resources to continue the day-to-day operations.

Your job as the owner is to focus on marketing and prospecting for more work. That means you have to trust that the person you put in charge has the skills, the dedication, and the desire to do everything in his power to guarantee that you make a profit and can continue to operate your business.

> Now imagine how it will feel knowing that your house, the one in which your family lives, will always be at risk, and that the way of life to which you and your family have become accustomed is riding on the success of your company.

My reason for this piece of on-the-job training is to prompt you to begin thinking like the owner of a contracting business. When you make the leap from being someone who just shows up to work and does what someone else tells you to do to being a foreman, your whole perspective has to shift as well. It's no longer enough to worry only about what you're doing today; now you need to worry about what your entire crew is doing. Do they have tools they need? Do they have the material they need? Do they have all of the pertinent information they need to do their job? While there is no easy way to prepare for this drastic change in thinking, some people make the shift more easily and naturally, while others struggle with their newfound responsibilities.

FINAL THOUGHTS

Using this book as a guide for becoming a great foreman and a successful leader starts by understanding the business basics behind the construction company. Your job is not simply "what you do for a living," but everything that goes on behind the scenes, and learning to look at things from the contractor's point of view is a valuable tool for seeing where you fit in your role as foreman.

When you accept the position of foreman for any project you automatically put yourself in the position of looking out for your company's best interests—and this is the perspective from which you need to approach your job. Frankly, if you don't see it this way you're probably better off declining the job altogether. I say this because I have seen too many foremen who, though they may understand what it takes to build the project because that is how they have been trained, don't take the time to learn all the other things they need to know. In fact many of them believe what they already know is *all* they need to know. Very few foremen take the initiative to know what goes on in the daily life of the owner of their company and how the owner is affected by the choices that they make out in the field.

This doesn't mean that you can't develop your own style and do things the way you think they should be done on the job site. But having insight into how a successful contracting business is run may help you see things in a way you've never seen them before. The more you understand the business, the better equipped you'll be to make important decisions, all of which will contribute to your chances of becoming a successful foreman.

Chapter 2

The Cost of Doing Business

Every construction contracting business carries financial burdens that remain somewhat hidden to those of us who work out in the field managing a project. These costs are part of the necessary expenses that allow your company to keep its doors open and complete the functions that both you and it performs. Keep in mind that when you are out on site running a project a distance from your company's office, your support staff, project managers, estimators, and many others of your team are working to support you while they continue to search out new projects and grow the company.

One of the most important things a foreman needs to know is that each dollar spent impacts the company's profitability.

Understanding the financial aspects of the company you work for in this way can change the way you think. Many foremen believe that as long as their project makes a profit, the company should be satisfied with their performance. The reality is that your company may be satisfied that your project did not lose money, but they know too well that making only a small profit on some projects while losing money on others won't pay the bills. It's up to you, the foreman, to do your absolute best to make sure that labor and money is not being wasted regardless of the size of the project.

A contractor's financial burdens fall into two distinct categories: *direct costs* and *indirect costs*, more commonly known as "overhead."

Direct costs are those costs incurred to actually build a project. These include, but are not limited to:

> » Material costs
> » Field labor, including fringe benefits
> » Portions of management expense
> » Equipment rental/insurance
> » Field offices/equipment
> » Storage units and space
> » Field vehicles
> » Permit fees

Indirect (overhead) costs are the contractor's numerous financial responsibilities necessary for performing its regular business functions, before the contractor can finally see a profit. All companies, large or small, have overhead costs relative to the size of the business. As a foreman, it's your job to strive to run efficient and productive projects in order to help your company offset these costs.

1. *Labor Overhead.* Labor overhead encompasses the salaries, wages and benefits of all employees and departments that *cannot* be charged directly to a specific project.

These include, but are not limited to:

» Owner/president	» Managers*
» Superintendents*	» General foremen*
» Estimators	» Marketing
» Purchasing	» Dispatch
» Payroll	» Human resources
» Receptionist	» Collections

> * Some projects may allow a portion of these costs to be charged to the job.

2. *Operations.* Operations costs include:

» Loan interest	» Legal fees
» Lease/rent/purchase	» Cell phone service
» Phone service	» Utilities
» Business insurance	» Vehicles, maintenance, gas, and insurance
» Business licenses	
» Office supplies	» Office equipment and maintenance
» Bonding	

I'll admit that it can be easy to forget about all the support staff continually working on your behalf back in your company's office quarters. After all, they're back there and you're out at the job site, and when you're out on a project you're busy with all the activities required to complete that project. It's not unusual for a foreman to visit his company's office only once or twice a year—or maybe not at all. But for this reason it's easy to remain unaware of the myriad tasks these individuals are doing to lay the groundwork so that you can do your job every day. Every time you send in time cards... every time you write a purchase order for material...every time you call your office to get more crew sent out to your job, you add one more task to someone else's list of things to do. We all need to recognize that these overhead employees who support you are just as important to your success as the people on your crew. Without them the business could literally not survive.

Most of us already understand the concept of overhead cost and how it is a part of any business. Having a firm understanding of how much money needs to be brought in just to keep your company's doors open, however, is another story. If your intentions are to become a successful foreman who might move on to become a project manager (or even a company owner), you will need to take *all* financial considerations into account every time you make a decision on every project you accept.

On-the-job Training: Financial Backing

In this brief exercise, I ask you to consider the company you are currently working for. First, estimate the number of support staff employees working at this company and their total concomitant salaries here: ____/____.

Then make a list of the approximate numbers of vehicles this company has on the road: ____.

Then add to that some of the other overhead items that we listed above: _____; _____;_____;_____.

Now do some rough math and total all of the above: _____. This number should give you some idea what it is costing your company to stay in business every day, week, month, and year.

Again, your estimate will be rough, but try to be as accurate as you possibly can. First of all, figure that the combined average wage of the company's support staff is somewhere around 70% of your yearly salary. When you total the vehicles in service, multiply by the lease payments, insurance, and gas for each one. These numbers are easily guestimated by gathering information from your own personal finances.

When you add together these two numbers of both staff wages and vehicles, you will have an approximate total of what your company spends over time. Are you surprised by the number you see before you? Has this exercise given you a more accurate perspective—even an appreciation—for the financial risk that your company takes every day in order to both provide you with an opportunity for employment and to attempt to make a profit itself?

The following chapter will discuss in more depth the many ways that contractors pay for their overhead costs and still manage to make a profit.

Chapter 3

How Contractors Make a Profit

MATERIALS MARK-UP

We all know that contractors mark up the materials they purchase for a project. But there are also labor costs related to the purchasing and handling of these materials as well as the cost involved in processing the billing of the materials. For this reason, although a company may mark up its material 10%, that doesn't mean it will clear 10% profit on that mark-up. Furthermore, on some projects the customer may choose to buy the big-ticket items himself, essentially removing the contractor's ability to make any money on the purchase of the item.

TIME AND MATERIAL PROJECTS

A time and materials project is one where the customer agrees to pay the contractor based on how many hours it actually takes to complete the project and how much material is used. This is not a blank check for the contractor to fill out! Most, if not all, of the time the customer writes a "not to exceed" clause into the contract for this precise purpose. As with material mark-ups, there are also administrative costs related to doing this kind of project, including a considerable amount of paperwork. In order to protect their interests, for example, most of the time customers require documentation regarding labor and material quantities used in order to authenticate that they are only paying for what is actually done on the project.

CHANGE ORDERS

Contractors often pick up extra work from the customer in the form of change orders throughout the course of a project. This work includes things the customer adds or items that were omitted on the original drawings on which the contractor based his original bid price. These changes are priced per change and are usually more profitable than the actual contract work. One reason is because the contractor's mark-up on a change order is generally higher than the mark-up used to originally procure the project where contractors may have lowered their "standard" mark-up during the estimating process in order to win the project. Naturally, if this is the case, they are hoping they can make any monetary deficiencies up in efficiency, production, and change orders. Another reason that change orders are more profitable is due to the fact that a crew will likely still be on site when the change order is issued, so there will be no additional costs involved with set-up, mobilization, and demobilization.

EFFICIENCIES

During the estimating process or at the start of a project, contractors dissect the project to search out those places where they might be able to reduce labor hours through efficiencies like prefabrication. For example, there are times when it may be more efficient and productive to build large quantities of like items in a shop, where they can be produced in a controlled and consistent environment. After production, these items are transported to the job site to be installed. Prefabrication helps the contractor bring down the overall per-unit cost by not having workers in the field building the items one by one.

There are a couple of advantages gained by working like this inside a shop away from the site: (1) the ability to order and stock larger amounts of material, potentially increasing the possibility of obtaining a discount from the supplier and (2) the ability to reduce labor hours by building these items in an assembly-line fashion. Without the need to frequently relocate workstations on site to allow for other trades to work in one area or another, many setbacks in production can be avoided altogether.

When deciding whether or not prefabrication would be beneficial for your project, ask yourself if what you are building will work in the field. If prefabricating the item will require a lot of adjustment or need to be taken apart on site then you'll end up losing more labor hours than you gained. And don't forget there will be costs associated with transporting and handling the prefabricated systems as you bring them to the job site as well. The important thing is to consider all the factors related to the prefab scenario before you jump into that state of mind. Whether prefabrication will pencil out in the end should be at the heart of your decision to move forward.

MARK-UP ON LABOR

As with material, contractors also mark up their labor costs. Again, administrative costs are tied to every employee a contractor has, so the contractor's mark-up never goes directly into the profit column.

PRODUCTION

At the heart of what really makes or breaks a contractor's chance of making a profit is production. Hypothetically speaking, if a contractor bids a project for 1,000 hours of labor, and it takes exactly 1,000 hours to complete the project, the only profit made is the mark-up that is left over after all overhead costs are removed.

If that same project is finished in 900 hours then there are 100 hours, plus the mark-up of those 100 hours, left on the table to help pay the company's overhead...plus a profit.

In theory, if a project were to use exactly the amount of hours for which it was bid and the materials used were exactly the same as estimated, the contractor would likely make a small profit.

If you only remember one thing from this book, however, remember this:

Production is the number one variable that can increase or decrease the profitability of any project you run.

As the foreman you can't change whether or not an expensive piece of equipment was left out of the estimate, but you can always affect how productive your crew is. I have been involved in more than a few projects where it became obvious something had been missed or left out of the estimate only after the project had begun. Although a bad situation, this is not always a death sentence for the project. A good foreman who plans well and runs an efficient crew can, at the very least, make sure that if the job loses money it is kept at an absolute minimum. But even those projects that are bid correctly or have a large profit margin built in have to be run with resolute efficiency.

At the end of the day it is the combined profits and losses of *all* the projects undertaken that defines the success of the company. Your success as a foreman will depend on your ability *to run the projects for which you are responsible* with the highest possible levels of efficiency and productivity.

Chapter 4

Production: Who Has the Biggest Impact?

The only possible answer to the question of who impacts production the most is the foreman. There is no other one individual who impacts a project's production, both positively and negatively, more than the on-site foreman. Just ask yourself: Does your project manager or company's owner come to your site every day to make sure that your crew is operating at maximum efficiency and production? Do either or both of them call you each day to ask you if you are doing everything you can to make sure your crew is as productive as they can be? If your answers are no and no then the answer is obvious: *you* have the biggest impact on production. Besides, if that is how owners and managers operated, why would they need you anyway?

Owners and project managers are too busy with other tasks to spend that kind of time watching over you and every other foreman's movements. In their minds, and rightfully so, you have been put in charge of the project, and as far as they are concerned you should be doing absolutely everything in your power to keep your job running smoothly.

When it comes down to it, you are the person who is accountable and will be held accountable. Your crew looks to you, their leader, for direction. If you leave too many questions unanswered or leave your crew without the material, tools, and information they need, the project is guaranteed to suffer. It's as simple as that.

Why is it so important that one person be responsible for having a thorough and concise plan, including the assignment of multiple tasks and the tools and materials necessary to complete them? Think about the alternative. Let's say you have a crew of 10 people and you leave it up to each individual to find something to work on, to purchase his own material, and to supply his own tools. How profitable do you think your project would be? What if you and your crew only had one set of prints to reference and had to take turns trying to figure out what they were going to do? Is it likely this project would run efficiently, let alone make a profit? I know these examples may sound basic, but the things I've witnessed in my career tell me that they need to be said.

For example, while working as a journeyman for someone else, I have often been in the position where my foreman has come to me, told me what he wants done, and then turned around and walked off—without first making sure that I had everything I needed to complete the task. Keep this in mind while you explore the following On-the-job Training segment.

On-the-job Training: Material Handling

Your foreman comes to you to lay you out (that is, to explain the details of a task he needs you to complete). After he gives you the information, you ask him if the material is on site. He tells you, "Well, I bought some a while ago...I'm sure the material is here somewhere; you'll have to look around and find it. Let me know if you don't find what you're looking for." And then off he goes.

While in principle this might work—you may eventually find the material you need—it would be a much more common scenario that you would find yourself on a wild goose chase, trying to scrounge up what you need and wasting all sorts of time doing it.

What mistake is this foreman making? First of all, it is the *foreman's* responsibility to have all the tools, material, and information the crew is going to need. Second, if the foreman explains a task to one of his crew and then walks away without knowing if he has what he needs, the foreman may never know how much time is being wasted while that person searches the job site for the materials the foreman "bought a while ago." I think we can all agree that it may not be glamorous, but the foreman still needs to be a material handler as much as he needs to be the person leading the crew. *Any time you force your crew to figure something out that you should have shared with them...any time you send them on a treasure hunt to try and find material or tools that should have been readily available to them...you are losing money for your company.*

Any time you force your crew to fend for themselves, you can be losing money for your company

---

I can hear the protests now. "I don't have time and I can't do everything. The crew needs to be responsible, too." And you're absolutely right that you can't and they should. But *you* are the one who orders material and *you* are the one who directs the crew. You are the one who signed on to do more than anyone else and they are the ones who signed on to help you do it. Your crew is only going to be as productive as you allow them to be. It falls on you to provide them with direction and the things they need to get the work done.

MAKING EXCUSES

I'm going to touch on something here that I'll be discussing in more detail later because, based on my experience and the attitudes of many foremen, I feel it's too important not to mention at this point.

Many foremen reading this book will now be saying the same thing, "I can't help it if when I buy material and stock the job with tools my crew misplaces them. I can't help it that they don't organize and take care of what I give them. I'd have to spend my entire day cleaning up after them to keep things organized and orderly." To which I say: That's unadulterated hogwash. It's simply not true.

Here's why. Your crew works *for you*. You direct them and you tell them what you need and expect from them. If you allow them to be slobs and abuse your tools and equipment then you have to take what you get. You can make excuses and point fingers all day long, but at the end of the day you are in charge, so it's you who are letting it happen.

You are not the only foreman thinking like this, however. Unfortunately, it's a common problem—but one that can be improved with a little knowledge and understanding of the benefits of thinking differently. That's why in Part 4, Chapter 21 we'll talk about communication skills and some of the tools that have worked for me to effectively put an end to this kind of predicament.

FINAL THOUGHTS

Running work isn't easy. It will take a big effort on your part to convey to your crew what is expected of them. This means you have to be willing to tell people what you want and expect and also be willing to confront and deal with those people who don't want to cooperate and do what you are asking them to do.

Chapter 5

Things That Hurt Production

Now that we know unequivocally that efficiency and production are the responsibility of the foreman, it's time to discuss some of the many external factors that can hurt production on any given project. Although it is true that every potentially problematic circumstance listed in this chapter lands at the feet of the foreman, every single one *can be overcome.* To do so, you may need to learn some new planning or organizational skills or improve your ability to communicate with and motivate others, but *you* are the only one who can truly identify your shortcomings in order to make the necessary adjustments and fix the situation.

Being the best foreman you can be means that you must always be on the lookout for new ideas and methods that will make your job easier and improve your chances for success. The day you think you know it all or become content with doing "just enough to get by" is the day you allow someone else to bypass you in your career. And we all know that those who continue to improve and learn from their mistakes are the ones who always rise to the top.

Below are the twelve most critical elements that can hurt production when the foreman is not doing the job he needs to do. (Most of these factors will be discussed in more detail in another chapter.)

1. *The foreman lacks a clear understanding of the business.* Are you a foreman who chooses not to have the proper number of tools or material quantities on a job because you think you're saving your company money? Before you answer, notice that I've used the word "chooses" because, as I've said, *every decision you make regarding efficiency and production on your project directly impacts your company's bottom line.* Always keep in the front of your mind that most of the things that affect efficiency and production *are within your power to change.*

On-the-job Training: The Screw Gun

You have at least one person on your crew who spends half an hour a day looking for a screw gun because you are one or two screw guns short of what you really need (and should have). How many hours that turn into wasted workdays does it take before you could have bought a new one?

For simplicity sake, let's say your employee costs your company $50 an hour.

At half an hour a day that equals $125 a week spent wandering the job searching for a screw gun. After three weeks, and $375 later, you could have bought a brand new drill that would have been available to your crew for the rest of the project and possibly for future projects. Either way, $375 has now been taken off the bottom line of your project. Think about the fact that if you were to let this continue for an entire year the total of lost income would now be a whopping $6,500!

When it comes to small tools and miscellaneous materials, the cost of paying for having what you need is minute in comparison to the cost for the hours of wasted labor when you don't have what your crew needs to do their work.

You can take this example and apply it to any item your crew might be looking for: a ladder, an extension cord, drill bits, or saw blades. How long will it take for someone wandering around looking for a drill bit or a roll of tape before you could have paid for it? *Don't skimp on the everyday things your crew is going to need. This is one of the most common and critical errors that many foremen make.*

Spending money hurts. I find it helps to recognize why it is so easy to get wound up about spending money on materials and tools. Obviously, these are costs that affect your project at the very moment that you make the purchase, and they can be painful. Because you know how much you are spending and because your company gets an invoice showing how much you are spending, it's natural to feel the impact. Unfortunately, labor does not work that way. Labor spent ineffectively often goes unnoticed until the end of the job is near, and by then it is impossible for anyone to put his finger on when and where the labor hours were wasted. It's like a leaky roof on your house. It might be years before you know the leak is there, but when you finally find it you have a big hole and lots of other damage to repair.

Things work the same way in the contracting business: when you finally find the leak (assuming you can or do find it) it is usually too late to do anything about it.

If your crew is wandering around the job site looking for tools and materials that should be readily available to them, you need to first recognize that you have a problem, then focus on finding a solution to get it fixed. It's easy to point the finger at the crew by insisting, "They don't put things away," and "They don't take care of the tools."

Although these statements may be true, it doesn't remedy the problem to keep repeating them. It has now become a communication problem between you and your crew. They need to understand that putting things away and taking care of the tools is part of their job and that it is the only way you run your projects. How will they understand? *The only way to be sure your crew knows what is expected of them is by communicating your expectations to them at the beginning of the project and every day thereafter.* Every day you ignore the issue and don't do something to remedy it, valuable hours are slipping away.

2. *Lack of planning.*

On-the-job Training: The Crew

Let's say you're running a project that needs more help, so you contact your shop to let them know you need to increase the manpower on your site. The next day your new crew-members show up to work. But instead of having their tools and materials ready for them so they can complete the task at hand, they spend most of the first day on their new job trying to get set up just so they can begin to be productive.

What is the cause of this inefficiency? You didn't take the time or make the effort to put together what they need in advance.

Planning in advance to have everything ready on the site is an important concern. Part of this planning effort needs to include having your new crew be familiar with the layout of the site and the location where all of your tools and material are staged. In this example, if you'd assigned someone familiar with the job—perhaps an apprentice—the task of rounding everything up for the new employees ahead of time, the crew would have been able to go right to work.

Finally, don't forget that when you treat your new employees in this manner you are sending the signal that they are not really welcome. This can contribute to a feeling that they are outsiders who are not being given the opportunity to be as productive as they would like to be.

3. *Lack of organization.* I find that when it comes to organization, it helps to think about the example you set for your crew. What they see you do will determine in their minds what you find acceptable. Keeping the prints, the trailer, or the work truck in shambles allows the crew to assume that organization is not one of your top priorities. Again, this speaks to the fact that—whether you like it or not—*you* are the person to whom they are looking for leadership. If they see that their leader doesn't mind working in a disorganized setting, then they won't work hard to stay organized. When and if you finally do come to your crew to ask them to be more organized and to take care the tools and materials, your credibility on this subject will have been seriously compromised.

It's simple. If you ask your crew to do something you obviously don't do, it just doesn't work. *You have to lead by example.*

Working together with your crew is the way to make this happen. Be part of the team when it comes to keeping all the tools and materials allocated and organized. Your crew should always be able to find the tools and materials they need within minutes. If you have multiple locations for storing material and tools, make sure that all similar items are stored together. If your crew has to go to three different locations to find all the different material they need to complete one task, labor is being wasted. Having everything your crew needs on site is not good enough; if they are not able to find what they need within a short period of time, production will go down. Soon their morale will follow suit.

4. *Lack of coordination.*

On-the-job Training: Coordination

Let's say you have to build a rack or mount a piece of equipment. Unfortunately, you failed to coordinate in advance with the other trades, who will also need space in the same area. What will be the result of your inaction?

Failing to coordinate your efforts or choosing not to look at the other trades' prints to see what they have going on only increases the likelihood that you will have some significant re-work coming your way.

It takes a lot less time to coordinate with the other trades and talk through a plan that works for all of you then it does to have to take something apart and rebuild it once it has already been installed.

5. *Lack of materials.*

On-the-job Training: Running Out of Materials

Imagine once again that you have a crew that is building pipe racks. For this purpose they will be putting up hundreds of feet of threaded rod and strut. Three days into their project they run out of nuts, washers, and other inexpensive materials. What happens now? That's right. Production comes to a halt.

Again, a halt in production means that you have not planned well enough and that your overall production will suffer for it. Sure, you might be able to borrow some from another trade temporarily, but it is still going to cost you time. The truth is that items like these are so inexpensive that there is no excuse for *ever* running out of them. If the crew building racks doesn't use them all, they are sure to be used later on in this project or on another project. *Remember, you'd have to buy a lot of nuts and bolts to make up for the hours of wasted labor that accrues by not having sufficient quantities in stock at all times.*

6. *Lack of tools.*

On-the-job Training: "Neither a Borrower Nor a Lender Be"

You're at the end of the project. The time has come where, in order to complete it, one of your tradesman is required to work in a ceiling at 12 feet. The tradesman gathers his tools and heads over to the spot. He stands beneath it and looks around. He's ready to begin—he has all the material and information necessary—but, low and behold, he has no way to reach the work area. What do you do?

This is yet another instance where borrowing a ladder from another trade might appear to be a viable option, but it's not a good one. The trade from whom you borrow this ladder will more than likely end up needing it back well before the tradesman is done with his ceiling project. That means that now you'll either have to switch gears, have your employee move on to another project, or go find another ladder, all of which will require him to re-tool and/or relocate. It's another costly miscalculation.

Being short the tools your crew needs is as costly as not having the material in the first place. Your crew can have the best intentions for completing a project in a timely manner, but you can't expect them to work magic if you tie their hands behind their backs by not providing what they need. Lack of tools or material hits you right where it hurts the most: in wasted and inefficient labor. *Never ask your crew to tackle a project unless you* know *they are going to have what they need to do their jobs.*

7. *Poor people skills.* We all know the expression "people skills," but what does it really mean? On the job site, it can mean communicating what you want and expect. It can also mean assessing your crew's strengths and weaknesses appropriately. Why? Because without proper assessment of your crews skills, production suffers. As a foreman you have to be able to put individuals in positions that best suit them, but that also suit your needs and will work to the project's advantage. Once you learn to identify the strengths and weaknesses of every individual on your crew, you can use that information to improve all aspects of their performance and the project's outcome.

For example, let's say you ask a crewmember to do something he may only have done a couple of times in his career. A worker in this position might feel unsure of his skill at the task, but say nothing. Certainly his work will progress more slowly and tentatively than you might wish. Plus, more significantly, is the fact that you will more likely than not end up with an unsatisfactory installation.

Take the time to make informed decisions.

Had you taken the time to ask this individual a few questions about his experience prior to putting him on the job, you could easily have surmised that what you planned to ask him to do was not his strong suit. At that point, you could have made an informed decision to give him more information to help him complete the task satisfactorily or chosen to have another employee do the job.

8. *Poor communication.* Your ability to communicate your thoughts and ideas to your crew is crucial to the success of your project. There are too many foremen who lack good communication skills and it costs them every single day. If you can't properly explain a project to your crew in exact detail, then how can you expect them to give you what you envision?

   There are many foremen who hurry through the laying out of a project or leave out valuable details only to get frustrated later when their crew do not do what they had in mind. Don't forget that every detail you leave out is one more detail left up to your crew's interpretation. At that point, how can you blame them for your dissatisfaction?

The only way to get exactly what you want is to explain exactly what you want.

Once you have done everything you can to outline your expectations, if you still find yourself unhappy with what your crew does then you have every right to be disappointed with them.

Remember, because you are the foreman you have unlimited access to the project's prints. You have also spent more time with them, dissecting the project piece by piece. To expect anyone on your crew to have anywhere near the knowledge of the project that you do is unrealistic at best.

Some foremen choose to not make the prints available to the people on their crew. Some just dole out small pieces at a time. Both are a huge mistake. Giving your crew access to the prints allows them to double check details and find answers to any questions that arise as they work. This saves you time and helps eliminate preventable mistakes.

9. *Poor crew morale.* Poor morale is the invisible production killer. A good foreman develops a sense for it, but it can easily go unnoticed either by choice or default. Poor

morale stems mostly from the lack of attention to the things mentioned above—people skills, communication, tools, material, and organization. Unfortunately, as we all know, a disgruntled crew often does not communicate its discontent with the foreman. Instead they commiserate amongst themselves when the foreman is not around, which only compounds the problem and often drags in other crewmembers who were previously otherwise content. As a foreman, you need to be aware of what causes poor morale, be able to recognize the signs, and know some ways to try to turn it around. It's helpful to know that many of the same things that hurt production also contribute to poor crew morale. When you have both, your project is in trouble.

On-the-job Training: Turning the Tables

Someone on your crew has shown up with the intention of being productive and doing a good job. Unfortunately, you haven't made what he needs available to him. Soon, this individual's attitude has quickly turned against you. You figure if you're lucky, he'll keep his dissatisfaction to himself. Unfortunately, because it is human nature to want to talk to other people and find out if they are having similar feelings and experiences, this will probably not be the case.

Who is to blame for the bad morale in this situation? Right—you, the foreman. Sure, there are people who will be negative no matter what you do for them, but you always have to give all your crewmembers the opportunity to do a good job for you. Let them see that you are working hard for them, too. Otherwise their thinking can go like this: "If my foreman doesn't seem to care about the job, then why should I?"

We've all been in this kind of a situation before, and it is a bigger problem than most of us care to acknowledge. So, don't let poor morale destroy the opportunity for your project to be successful.

Keep your attention tuned into the mind set of your crew. This way if you see it start to change you can do something about it.

---

10. *Crew inconsistency.* It is the nature of construction that you will constantly be required to switch gears and change direction throughout the project to its completion. One by-product of this constant maneuvering is that it's difficult to find a consistent path during most phases of a project and to complete those phases from start to finish. During these transitions, many different people will be working on any single phase of the job. But having one of your crewmembers pick up where someone else leaves off creates the opportunity for important details to be missed. That means it's up to you to fully communicate the nature of the work originally given to the person who started the project. Otherwise, you're opening the door for a step to be skipped, a mis-

take to be made, or a loose end to be created and potentially left untied.

It is also in the nature of construction that projects go through cycles of being busy and slow. This means that crewmembers who worked with you in the beginning of the project may not be with you in the end. This situation occurs naturally when they leave to work on other projects when they're not needed on yours. Soon they'll be valuable to the foreman on their current job. When you want them back it may be difficult, if not impossible, to get them to return. That's why having a crew that has been around for most of the project is a big advantage to you. A crew that has been around since near the beginning of the project is much more likely to understand the big picture. Bringing in workers who are unfamiliar with the project in the end only equates to less than optimum production.

If this scenario is unavoidable, the best way to attack this problem is by having very clear and concise projects for any new workers to complete. Have all the necessary tools and material set up exactly where they need it—in their work area. It's also good idea to have them work with or around someone who has been working on your project long term because this person will be able to answer simple questions and help them find anything they might need.

Talk to your crew. Again we need to broach the topic of communication, this time in this context of new crewmembers. New crewmembers will always have questions and concerns as they work through a task. If you identify a member of your current crew as the go-to person for answers and direction, it is your responsibility to communicate this fact with that individual. Generally, this person will not mind helping you out. But if new crewmembers suddenly show up asking questions and this individual's own work slows down, frustration is sure to be the outcome.

Therefore, always start by asking if this member of your crew is willing to help you out. Let him know that you are acknowledging his importance to you and the fact that his production may go down slightly as he attends to the various questions that arise.

There are those who will feel that taking on the role of being responsible for others and providing answers means they should be compensated for the extra time and duties. Sometimes this is an option and sometimes it is not. That's why you should take nothing for granted. Always ask first before pushing responsibilities on others.

11. *Avoidable mistakes and re-work.* Mistakes and re-work go hand in hand. That's why mistakes and incorrect installations only mean one thing: a huge negative impact to the bottom line. Any time you have someone working to take something apart in order to re-install it correctly, the hours being spent are going directly into the red column. This is why it is so important to focus on every detail of the project as it comes together.

Sometimes mistakes do not become apparent until later in the project when they are much more difficult to correct. Of course not all mistakes are unavoidable. They happen under the best of circumstances. Therefore, it is the nature of your position that you stay focused on your responsibilities and plan well to keep them to an absolute minimum.

On-the-job Training: Long Leads

An order for a long lead item has been placed incorrectly. This is one of those times when you recognize there has been an avoidable mistake. Unfortunately, in this case the fix may not be so easy because the order that was placed was for a custom item that had to be made specifically for your project. This means the item has to be re-ordered and you're going to be stuck waiting for the replacement.

The result? Not only can't you finish the project, but you foresee two other problems: (1) you're going to be in hot water with the customer *and* (2) you're going to have to take responsibility for the cost of the incorrectly ordered item.

Do you recognize now that spending a little extra time yourself or having someone else proof your orders for correctness would have lessened the chance that this kind of situation would occur?

Re-work. Now let's talk about re-work. Buildings like hospitals or places of assembly require unique installation methods and have their own special code requirements. These need to be thoroughly researched by you so they can be correctly implemented. The intended use of a building will influence which materials can be used, establish requirements for egress in the event of an evacuation, and designate many other trade specific requirements.

If you and/or your crew undertakes an installation based on assumptions rather than the required specifications or code regulations for that project, you could easily find yourself tearing out your hair along with what you installed in order to start over. Is rework a common occurrence? Unfortunately, yes. Fortunately, it's also preventable most of the time.

12. *Loose ends.* Having too many loose ends at the end of a project can be one of the most frustrating and pressure-filled experiences a foreman will ever experience.

On-the-job Training: Completion

You're facing the end of your project. You're trying to finish and move out. But things you either forgot weren't finished or tasks that you neglected because you thought you would have time to finish later start cropping up. Meanwhile, the general contractor, your company, and the customer aren't looking for excuses. They want you done and out of the building. Soon. Now.

This is the kind of pressure nobody needs or wants. That's why good planning techniques and good note-taking skills can guide you through the project in a way that avoids many of the potential loose ends altogether.

When you let loose ends slip through the cracks during the completion of a project, you'll end up with a real profit killer in the end. Any extra hours you may save through efficiency and production slowly wither away as your crew spends hours and hours trying to first identify the loose ends and then try to finish them. This might be as simple as making a label or it may involve ordering more of some material that you were sure you weren't going to need.

Loose ends are a part of construction. It is impossible to eliminate all of them. The nature of construction is that you work on different parts of the project in phases, starting and stopping them multiple times to allow other trades to do their portion of the tasks. The key to loose ends is making sure that everything that can be finished is finished while one of your crewmembers is working on it. If you do pull somebody off a project before it's finished, keep a thorough record of what still remains to be done. Then, as soon as possible, go back and tie up every single incomplete thread.

Loose ends; loose lips. Where does communication enter into our loose ends framework? That's easy. Communicate with your crew. Regularly. Let them know that you need their help with whatever loose ends appear. Ask them to keep you updated about any loose ends that are left behind when they are taken from a task that they might otherwise have completed. Tell them that you want to know if they don't have the materials or tools they need to complete their task...that you want to hear from them. Most of the time, all you have to do is ask.

The remedy to loose ends: Stay in constant communication with your crew and be clear about what you need.

FINAL THOUGHTS

Ultimately it is the foreman's responsibility to make sure that loose ends don't stack up. It's easy to shift the blame to your crew for loose ends as it is for anything else, but bear in mind that your crew works for you. More often then not the people working for you are only doing what you've asked of them.

Chapter 6

Financial Matters

As a foreman, you shouldn't have to worry about the day-to-day financial needs of your company.

Sounds good, doesn't it? But not needing to worry about these financial needs doesn't mean you shouldn't at least have a basic understanding about what they are and why they matter. One of my primary reasons for including this chapter is to help dispel some myths about contractors and their finances.

The other reason is that I know many foremen who hold a strong and sometimes destructive belief that their company is making more money than it actually is, an attitude that often leads to resentment and discontent. Discussing some fundamental financial aspects of the contracting business will therefore help every foreman out there who wants to do the best job he can.

MISINFORMATION

Since the beginning of my career I've noticed that many individuals working in this field have significant misconceptions about their company's financial status and are convinced that every contractor is cash rich and making huge profits on the backs of their employees.

It's time to burst this bubble. The fact is that in most cases this is simply not true. That's why I feel the need to restate here, at the risk of being obvious, that the primary objective of any contracting business is *to make a profit*. Although most of the people making this assumption speak freely and without any kind of valid information, they do appear to have an objective for spreading the misinformation they share.

Let me explain. Have you ever known someone who complains just to complain? Someone who thinks he deserves more compensation than he's getting? Without even knowing the true ins and outs of a company's financials, it's easy to see how someone like this would feel justified in jumping to unfounded conclusions—and sharing them with others.

On-the-job Training: Contracts

You are the foreman running a project for your company. You know that the contract awarded to your company is for $2,000,000. The project could take a year, be labor-intensive, and take the majority of the $2,000,000 to complete, but from your point of view (uninformed though it is), the company appears well situated to make a lot of money. Although you are unaware of the financial details of the project, you feel under-appreciated and resentful.

It's easy to become focused on the contract amount of a project and lose sight of what it's actually going to cost to build it. In this sense, I believe that if companies gave their foremen weekly cost reports and involved them more in some of the business aspects of construction many misunderstandings would be corrected, most before they ever begin. Knowing the scope of the company's real financial burdens can help the foreman be realistic and put his focus back on the project—and keep it there.

FINANCIAL REPORTS

Companies often request the foreman's input to complete a form every month in an attempt to determine the project's overall status. The company then turns the form into a job progress report used in forecasting the company's financial needs in the months to come. Most of the reports I have seen include material costs incurred up to that point, labor hours used, and the total labor hours still available.

Unfortunately, these forms and reports don't always explain the whole story.

To help you understand the big picture, you really need to see your project's expenses in dollars, including daily, weekly, and monthly amounts. Making these costs known is the first step. The second step would be for your company to reveal some information about its overhead costs in order to provide you with a larger perspective. I am not suggesting that your company reveal every invoice for every utility, lease, and so on. But armed with more information and education, you will be better equipped to make informed decisions. This means everyone wins. When you are part of a team of people who are all aware of the common challenges and goals, both the company and the project stand a better chance of running efficiently.

PROFIT AND RISK

Though this next suggestion may be unwelcome, I'm going to risk saying it anyway because it needs to be said. Because the contractor is the only one taking a risk in order to make a profit, it is my opinion that the contractor is the one that deserves to make whatever profits are possible on any project it undertakes.

I'll explain. When a contractor takes on a project, there is no guarantee that there will be a profit. Contractors have to hope that they've thought of everything during the estimating process and that their foreman is going to manage the project skillfully. This goes back to what we talked about in Chapter 1 about trying to imagine what it feels like to be the only one taking a financial risk. When you work as a foreman you get your paycheck frequently enough that you'd know really quickly if your company stopped paying you. You budget your personal life based on the amount and frequency of your paydays. Contractors don't have that luxury. They have to make educated guesses and hope nothing goes wrong.

Does it sound as if I'm only looking at things from the contractor's point of view? If so, I can only say that it really does benefit you as a foreman to understand these aspects of the business. Just as you wouldn't want your company to discount the skills and abilities you bring to the table, the company doesn't want you to discount what it is providing you. When you take on the position of foreman, you are entering into a mutual agreement with your company that requires a commitment from both of you. If the two of you cannot come to a mutual understanding to your satisfaction, then you shouldn't take the position. If you are not happy with the compensation you are receiving your commitment to the project will be severely undercut.

A great foreman makes the company's primary objective his primary objective, too. If you believe you aren't being compensated the way you'd like and you feel the company isn't offering you the extra incentives you think you deserve, the message is clear: decline the position.

REALITY

It would be naïve to think that every single project a company chooses to take on will be profitable. Though that is certainly the goal, the nature of the construction industry and its many variables makes it a goal nearly impossible to accomplish. Sooner or later every contractor takes on a project that for one reason or another loses money. Perhaps the loss hinges on incorrect estimates or unforeseen circumstances...or the foreman's lack of efficiency. But whatever the reason the contractor has to make up those losses somewhere else—or be forced to close the doors.

At the risk of being redundant, running a job well and coming in under budget does not necessarily mean your company has made a huge profit. With overhead costs and losses from other projects, it is entirely conceivable that your company is barely breaking even.

The point is that you really have no way of knowing the company's financial status—unless the company discloses it to you. The answer is simple.

Do the best job you can every time. Your solid effort will make it much more likely that your company will be—and stay—successful.

WHEN DOING IT RIGHT ISN'T ENOUGH

There are always times when no matter what you do it doesn't feel like enough. Speaking from experience, one of those times is when you know you are doing everything possible to run an efficient and productive project, only to hear that some other foreman across town is running his project into the ground. Learning that other foremen aren't putting in the same effort you are can make your efforts feel futile and make you feel frustrated.

I have been on larger projects where multiple foremen are in charge of various parts of the job. It doesn't take long before it becomes very clear which foremen are good planners and which are not. Some will be constantly roaming the project scrounging for material or tools out of other foremen's areas. These are foremen who use their counterparts who plan well as a crutch. After all, the foremen who plan well always have what they need for their crew and can be relied on in a crunch.

If you ask one of our not-so-good planners why they don't have what they need, you'll usually hear, "Hey, we're all on the same team, right? We all work for the same company, right? We all need to work together." We all know this is true, and we all know the project is a team effort. But when one person shirks by not planning so that his work is inefficient, that person serves to drag the whole team down. That's why if you are not planning and scheduling far enough in advance that you rarely have to borrow material and tools from another crew, it is up to you to correct this inequity.

Being a foreman requires that you supply *everything* your crew needs. Any time you haven't planned in advance takes away potential profits for your company. Simple, but true nonetheless.

CASH FLOW

In almost all cases contractors have to purchase materials and pay their employees far in advance of when they will be reimbursed for these expenses. Typically companies do not receive payment for up to 90 days after a project-related expense is incurred. I'll explain how this works.

Generally speaking, when contractors are awarded a project there are no payments made up front. This means that due to the initial costs involved with estimating the project and getting the project underway contractors have to operate using any working capital they have from previous projects or resort to borrowing money from a lender to get the project going.

The contractor signs an agreement with the general contractor or customer that spells out exactly how much can be billed, and when, throughout the length of the project.

During the first month, the contractor does not bill the customer at all. During the second month, the contractor bills the customer based on the expenses incurred during the first month of work, including material, labor, administrative expenses, and a small percentage for profit. During the third month, the contractor expects to receive a payment for what was billed for the first month of work. This cycle repeats over and over again until the project is finished.

It's clear, therefore, that the contractor will be out quite a bit of money at any given time. And by the time the payment for what was done during the first month is received, the project has probably ramped up to more employees and the need for more tools and material. Therefore, the payment for the first month will not cover the new expenses of the third. This means that during the entire project the company is always behind relative to the money it has put out versus the money it has been paid. As the project begins to wind down, although the payments received become larger than the expenses incurred, the contractor may still be in the red.

Remain focused! Do not allow yourself or your crew to coast to the finish line.

Furthermore, at the end of the project the customer can hold the final payment back if dissatisfied about whether the contractor has fulfilled all commitments. Generally, this final payment is where any profits that are made are finally realized. This makes the end of the project very important. Any of those loose ends or punch-list items that have not been finished are the very items that can keep your company from receiving its final payment.

RISK VERSUS REWARD

Take a minute to think about the amount of risk your company takes in order to receive a reward for their efforts. In discussing the cash flow of a project it probably became clear to you that any profits your company stands to make are not only delayed during the project, but are purely hypothetical until every requirement of the contract has been completed to the customer's satisfaction and the company receives its final payment.

Contractors accumulate profits through the volume of work their company performs. At least this is the case for larger commercial/industrial contractors that take on many projects and attempt to make a small profit on each one. For every project that does well there may be one that does not. This is why every single foreman is critical for any company's success. The concept of making a profit based on volume doesn't work if you have only half of your foremen running efficient and productive jobs.

LARGE PROJECTS VERSUS SMALL PROJECTS

When a small project is not run efficiently and requires more labor hours to complete than were bid into the project, the percentage of losses increase dramatically for every hour that you run over.

On-the-job Training: Bidding Concerns

When a project that is bid for 100 hours goes over by 10 hours, it is 10% in the red. But when a project bid for 1,000 hours goes over by 10 hours, it is only 1% in the red. Even though the dollars related to both are the same, the impact in terms of how you and your company see the loss will be different. If you run a few jobs in a row that come in at 10% over for labor, you'll probably need to prove yourself again before further opportunities will be presented to you. On the other hand, if you have a few jobs that come in only 1% over, your employer will be less likely to analyze your abilities with as much scrutiny.

Also, just because a job loses money, your company is not necessarily going to assume you did a bad job. Typically, the company will pull everyone who was involved with the project together, including the project manager and estimator, and try to figure out where the problems were.

When you run smaller projects there is very little room for errors, re-work, or other oversights that result from poor planning and organization. Small projects require you to mobilize your tools and material, something that takes time and energy. Small projects do not offer you the ability to ramp up slowly to different phases of the project the way large projects do, so that you have what you need precisely when you need it. That's why you need to think of everything ahead of time. If you build it in your head before you ever get started you'll avoid many of the seemingly constant starts and stops that can occur when you haven't planned out the details.

Large jobs do have some advantages. One is the ability for the contractor to negotiate the prices he pays on large quantity items. Since small price breaks are sometimes available based on volume purchases, the company has the option of getting quotes from multiple vendors.

Large jobs also have their own challenges, however. For example, let's say you have a project that requires a general foreman who will be responsible for three other foremen. Of the three foremen, one is very well organized and always has what his crew needs. The second foreman plans pretty well, but doesn't always focus on the material and tools portion of his planning. The third foreman can't be bothered with the demands of planning and ordering. He claims that flying by the seat of his pants is his "style."

Will it be surprising when these foremen and their crews begin bickering over tools and material? When the foreman who has planned out and has what he needs constantly finds himself in the position where he has to lend tools and material to the other two foremen? When he and his crew are frustrated because they are now left short and in the lurch—even though they were better prepared?

When you hear the argument that "It's a team effort," and "We should all be able to share tools, right?" it's time to look at the facts. A real team effort means that each foreman is taking care of his own responsibilities for his crew.

If the project is at risk because lack of responsibility has become a constant theme, it is time for the general foreman to step in and straighten it out.

FINAL THOUGHTS

Understanding the realities of the finances of contracting can solidify the importance of your role in your company's success. Don't forget that your company is providing you with an avenue for you to use your leadership and management skills to provide for you and your family. Whenever a contractor goes out of business, the result is that we all have one less place to find employment.

PLANNING

Chapter 7

Planning: Your Top Priority

THIS IS WHERE IT ALL STARTS

Learning to plan means learning to organize. Once you know how to do both, your competence will inspire and motivate your crew to succeed. Furthermore, knowing what goes into thorough and detailed planning—in other words, what you should be doing and when you should be doing it—will help lessen your stress and boost your confidence every time. Doors will open and opportunities will present themselves.

The foremen who truly understand what it takes to consistently be successful are few and far between, however. If there's one thing I've learned in the construction industry it's that if you apply yourself and pay attention to detail you'll always have a job and you'll always be given opportunities. The truth is that contractors need people like you. They need someone who is willing to protect their interests as if they were their own.

Keep this in mind as you are out there running a project for your company. *They need you just as much as you need them.* They are entrusting you with their money and their reputation. If you take care of them, they'll take care of you.

THE IMPORTANCE OF PLANNING

It has always seemed obvious to me that a foreman in the construction industry, simply by virtue of his job, would have to understand the importance of planning. That's why I've been surprised to see that this hasn't proven to be the case. Though I believe most everyone objectively knows it's good to plan, over the last 20 years I've met very few foremen who have revealed a true inclination to explore or apply good planning techniques.

GOOD PLANNING

What exactly is "good planning"? In brief, good planning is thorough. It is detailed. And it leaves very little to chance or misinterpretation.

The majority of foremen believe it is enough to look through the prints a little every day and take note of some of the various tasks that will need to be addressed (at some point). But frankly, if this is your idea of planning you are most likely spending most of your time in a reactionary mode dictated by what the other trades around you are doing. You'll know if this is the trend when you find yourself reacting to things as they come up rather than approaching the day with an educated and decisive plan that anticipates what might happen and when. *If this is the status quo, there is no possible way your project is running efficiently.* Every time you have to react rather than carry out a planned attack on a particular project you are losing efficiency and production.

GOOD PLANNING AND GOOD FOREMEN

Here's the thing. A lot of foremen manage to skate by with poor planning skills, somehow finding a way to eke out a small profit and convince their project managers that they're doing a good job. But this fact doesn't compensate for the other side of the coin: that without the thorough planning that allows you to work out the inevitable kinks, you will never be able to run a job at maximum efficiency and production.

The construction industry is littered with mediocre foremen who bounce from contractor to contractor, leaving a trail of poorly managed jobs in their wake. Many of them have developed pretty good sales pitches to go with the overinflated self-image of their true capabilities. To a contractor in the market for a new foreman, the exaggerated claims made by the new prospect probably sound pretty enticing. But the charade only lasts for so long when the foreman proves to be unable to produce the results he promised.

I have seen it many times. A new foreman comes along who thinks he has it made because he got the opportunity to run a job or because a couple of his projects have gone smoothly. But long-term multiple successes are the only way to be labelled "successful" in a contractor's eyes. If a contractor detects a lack of desire and motivation to maximize the company's profitability, you may end up on the short list of people to replace—fast.

The construction industry is no different from any other in that continued employment is tied to success; in this case, to the success of the projects you run. And, as in any other industry, there will always be someone in your rear view mirror looking for you to slip up so they can pass you by.

PLANNING AHEAD

The first thing to know about planning is that there is no starting point and no finish line. From the very first day of the project until the very last, a foreman has to be thinking about what's coming down the road and the best way to accomplish it. If you aren't doing some kind of planning every day then there will come a time during the project when you realize that you should have been planning for that day.

Sure, some things are hard to plan for, but let those things be the exception, not the rule. If common types of emergencies typically come up for your trade during the course of a construction project, have a plan in place to handle them. For example, if you are in the electrical trade and in charge of temporary power and lighting, make sure to have extra material on site in case there is a sudden need for more of either one.

JUMP IN!

When you make the jump from working in the field and being led to leading others, the way you look at your responsibilities has to change. In the past, your whole career as an apprentice and a journeyman was about showing up on time, being reliable, and being as productive as possible every day. Most of your day-to-day projects were likely a day to a few days' long. But even as a journeyman or apprentice you had to do some planning because if you didn't you would have found yourself stopping constantly to get more material or to fix something that you installed incorrectly. If this was the case it only stands to reason that you would not have been successful at any of your jobs...which means you would not be standing here today with the chance at an opportunity for the position of foreman.

Since you are here reading this book, we can assume that you have indeed been successful as an apprentice and journeyman and that you have earned your promotion to foreman. The shift will come in learning to think ahead for your entire crew as opposed to yourself alone, and to anticipate what your crew will need to stay productive. This attitude of constant anticipation needs to become your norm.

I'm the first to admit that it can be a difficult transition to go from the mind set of a worker to the mind set of a foreman. There will be times when you'd rather jump right in and join your crew. Some jobs will support your preference, but others will not. The important thing to recognize is that if you spend your time out on the job site working instead of planning, all you're doing is setting yourself up for a time down the road when you and your crew won't be prepared. When that happens, you'll all be scrambling around trying to get something done without the proper tools and materials. Plus, whatever production you might have gained by working with the tools earlier will now be entirely lost...and more.

This can be a tough lesson, especially for those individuals who are really motivated to be productive and like the challenges of working in the field, but it's well worth the effort.

FINAL THOUGHTS

...One last thing. I can pretty much guarantee you that you will never hear a foreman say he wished he hadn't planned something out so well. What you *will* hear is the lament of the foreman who's wishing he spent more time building a detailed plan after something has gone wrong.

Chapter 8

Planning in Advance

PLANNING YOUR TIME

Detailed planning starts with planning in advance. Even for shorter-length projects, two to three weeks ahead is necessary and should include tasks that might take as little as an hour to those that might take a week or more to complete.

Planning ahead starts with making a list. Keep in mind that by "list" I really mean a detailed *written* assessment of tasks that you know need to be done and you know can be done. Random projects that are rattling around in your head don't cut it. After all, how will it help you if you have to assign crewmembers a new task on short notice because they are unable to complete the work you had planned for them?

Your list should include all the information (layout), tools, and material to ensure the specific tasks on your list will be accomplished;

to have a list of tasks to complete without everything on site and readily available that you need to complete the task is a waste of time. Making a list is more than simply a way to jot down the elements of a task, however. Every moment of your pre-planning provides another opportunity for exposing potential problems and finding alternative solutions before they occur.

ONGOING PLANNING

Planning doesn't start and stop with a list either. Continuous, ongoing planning for the later stages of the project is also a necessity, whether for long lead items or items that will require coordination with other contractors. Try to avoid getting so caught up in day-to-day issues that you aren't thinking far enough into the future about the later phases of the project.

As issues, questions, or long lead items come up while you're looking through the prints or during coordination meetings, write these things down. As soon as you can, begin the process of getting questions answered and the items ordered. Don't forget: when you are a foreman you will constantly be bombarded with questions and concerns all day long. To think that at the end of the day you are going to remember every conversation you've had is unrealistic, and it's much too easy to forget something if you don't write it down. The reality is that if you wait until the work day is over to try to remember the issue so you can write it down, there is a good chance you won't do it at all.

TAKING ACTION ON YOUR PLAN

So, you've made a list. Probably more than one by now, if you're anything like me, and they just keep growing. The important thing to remember is that a list that stays in your pocket is nothing more than a piece of paper with scratches on it. After a day or so it will get mixed in with other loose papers and will then probably get lost all together. When you find it—*if* you ever find it—the time will have passed for you to do what needed to be done, that is if you can even read the scraps you scrawled in the first place.

Not only do you need to have a system for keeping your notes and staying on top of all of the things that come at you throughout the day, but you have to decide how to take action on all the things you're adding to your continuously updating list. Choosing not to write things down means only one thing: that you will be blindsided by problems that could have otherwise been avoided. As we know, operating from a reactionary mode is one example of how a project can lose valuable labor hours, but it also reveals why many foremen believe they are hit with so many surprises.

COMPLACENCY

When you agree to be the foreman on a project, you commit to doing everything in your power to make sure it will be run as efficiently and productively as possible. Without the appropriate mind set and understanding of the role you've taken on, however, it's possible to be lulled into complacency as you tackle the problems that crop up every day rather than spend the necessary time to put a solid plan in place.

But allowing yourself to fall into this way of thinking only makes it more difficult to complete a job on time or under budget. It's true that lots of the people who run work continually make a small profit, but if those same people took a different approach to planning and organizing they would see their project's profit margins increase significantly.

FINAL THOUGHTS

You were given the opportunity to be a foreman due to your hard work and knowledge of your trade. Apply the same approach and attitude to your new job as project leader and into the field when you work with other foremen.

Chapter 9

Failure to Plan

Is your crew standing around waiting for you to figure out what they should do next? If so, you should be cringing at the sight. Is it because you're waiting on another trade or because you don't have the tools or material? Is it because you don't have enough work planned out in advance for the size of crew you have working for you? Whatever the reason, the crux of the matter is that a failure to plan yields consequences. That's why in this chapter we'll be exploring what some of these consequences are and how they directly affect you and your project.

UNPRODUCTIVE DOWN TIME

When another trade changes your direction it's easy to take the attitude that it's because of them that you can't do what you planned. If this is truly the case then this is something you, as the foreman, need to take up with the other contractor. But it still does not justify having nothing for your crew to do at any given time.

Don't forget that once those hours are gone you can't get them back. Having a good contingency plan in place is exactly what will enable you to handle this type of situation and keep you from losing valuable hours.

Furthermore, other trades will rarely be held responsible for slowing your crew down. Sure, there are always the threats of back-charging a contractor for making another trade change direction or slowing another trade down, but in my experience threats like these seldom lead to any money changing hands.

CONFLICT

Do the challenges you face on the job dictate the productivity of your project? There are always going to be those times when what you had planned for your crew doesn't pan out. This can be due to conflicts with other contractors or any number of unforeseen problems. Remember, this is simply the nature of construction. But, again, it is the foreman's responsibility to make sure when something happens there is always something productive waiting in the wings for his crew.

This is the perfect time to take out that list of short projects you've been keeping with you. Start one or two up and then take the extra time to assess your options for the next best one to begin.

Remember, any production is better than none at all.

UNNECESSARY RE-WORK

If you pay attention to detail, coordinate with other trades, and communicate the information thoroughly to your crew you should have a minimum amount of re-work. It therefore makes sense that most re-work comes from not paying attention to details when the work is being planned out. One aspect of good coordination and layout is looking at all the prints from front to back and taking the other trades into consideration relative to what they'll need to do their job.

After you have a detailed idea of the work your crew will be doing, communicate it to them thoroughly and leave no room for misinterpretation. How do you know when there is mutual understanding? When you have not only explained the task, but you continue to constantly check in with them to confirm that they understand—and are in agreement—with everything you're asking them to do on an ongoing basis. Having them repeat your instructions back is one way to catch anything that may have a tendency to slip through the cracks.

Everybody knows that a picture is worth a thousand words. On the job site, taking a minute to provide a quick sketch to describe the task, including dimensions, materials, and any other pertinent information, can delineate what your words may have not. A sketch also makes a good reference tool should a crewmember forget a detail and want to refer back to it for clarification. Time spent in this way is well worth the extra effort on your part.

Don't forget: Projects never include re-work hours; therefore, those hours go directly into the red column.

POOR CREW MORALE

We've talked a little bit about how the morale of your crew is critical to your project's success and how poor morale can be devastating to its outcome. But did you know that there are many ways to influence crew morale without speaking a word?

Since the number-one driver of poor morale in the construction industry is not having everything needed to do the job, it only follows that good morale can be helped by supplying the necessary tools, material, and information for the project. Contrary to popular belief, most people who come to work want to be productive and do a good job to earn their paycheck. When they have what they need, they work with motivation and efficiency. Take that opportunity away and they'll begin to lose interest—quickly. Once they lose interest, it only goes downhill from there.

It is very common on a typical construction site to hear, "The foreman doesn't care if we have what we need, so why should we care about being productive?" Even if the truth is that you, the foreman, do care, if your caring is not concrete—that is, you're not giving your crew what they need—then your actions will be speaking much louder than your words.

Be prepared at all times and lead by example. Your crew will see your commitment to the project and to their continued success.

LOSS OF PROFITS

It almost goes without saying that a poor bottom line will get more attention than anything else when review time rolls around. That's why making a profit for your company should be one of the driving forces behind your making planning a priority.

It's a simple equation. Your company's ultimate goal is to make a profit. When you don't plan well profitability is the first thing that goes out the window. Although not every project can or will make a profit (due to the many different variables involved), the potential loss or gain of profits is always directly related to how well you do your job—in other words, how well you plan and manage your project.

On the projects that don't have much chance to make a profit, a good foreman can still minimize the losses incurred by his company by planning well and running an efficient crew. This approach is just as valuable to your company as turning in a large profit on a project that has larger profit margins built in. Remember this bit of wisdom when you take on a project that has obvious problems. The project still needs to be completed and the better you manage it the better it will be for you and your company.

PENALTIES

Profits are never a sure thing. Losing profits due to penalties incurred when a project runs over schedule hurts you and the company. Particularly on many larger projects, if a contractor fails to meet deadlines spelled out in the contract penalties will be assessed upon the completion of the job. For the foreman who struggles with anticipating the direction of the project, who finds himself behind schedule, and who is forced to play catch-up throughout the entire job, penalties and lost profitability is the unfortunate outcome.

As mentioned earlier, although back charges from other trades are rarely enforced or paid, it is not uncommon for a contractor to lose profits due to his foreman's poor planning. Furthermore, in cases where you've fallen behind in the project and are unable to make schedules and where your poor timing has ended up affecting the other trades and their ability to complete their own installations, the other trades may not be so understanding. In fact, trades that are unable to proceed with their work and can prove it was because you didn't finish a phase of work according to the established schedule may think again about back charging your company for their resultant decreased efficiency and production.

LOSS OF CONFIDENCE

Self-esteem is not the subject of this book. But losing confidence in your own ability to do the job is the kind of loss that can have lasting consequences that stay with you throughout your career. To understand why something like this might occur, let's look at what typically happens when an individual takes on the role of foreman.

If you are in the position where you've been chosen to work as a foreman for your company, it's likely that you have some kind of history with them. Maybe you've completed your apprenticeship with them or maybe you came to work for them a bit later in your career. Either way, you have shown them something that made them believe you had what it takes to move to the next level. Just the fact that you've been asked to be a foreman should tell you that your company recognizes your hard work and dedication and sees you as much more than just an average employee.

So, where's the catch?

The down side to being promoted is that this new role will be much more of a challenge. After being successful in the earlier stages of your career and confident in your work, you've taken on a new role in which you might not be immediately successful. Speaking from experience, it can really mess with your head when you go from being well liked and well respected as a worker to being constantly in the line of fire for your lack of ability as a foreman.

What you need to remember is that becoming a good foreman is a process, not an overnight shift. You might compare it to going through another apprenticeship, only this time most of the training is on the job and there's no instructor. It can take years to understand what it takes. To be honest, I've worked for many long-time foremen who still don't really get it.

You will develop your own style over time, but it is important in the beginning to learn from other foremen who are clearly successful in the field. I think you'll find that one of the things that makes these foremen so successful is their attention to the planning process.

LOSS OF CREDIBILITY

Credibility is something you earn. You earn it when you follow through on your promises to your crew, other trades, and the customer, and when you make good on the commitments you make to your company. If you make promises you fully intend to keep but constantly come up short, you will soon lack credibility with your peers. On the other hand, people tend to understand if on occasion something happens that's out of your control and causes you to miss a deadline or a commitment. If normally they know they can count on you to walk the walk, not just talk the talk, they will generally be more than willing to cut you some slack. As long as you continue to tell them the truth, not just what they want to hear, and as long as you are sincere and have established a track record for being credible, you are much more likely to receive leniency. With that said, the construction industry is full of people who promise the world with no intention of backing up their promises with action.

Credibility is built one step at a time, one job at a time, and follows you throughout your career. Like respect, credibility is a lot harder to gain than it is to lose. If you work hard at it and keep it in the forefront of your mind at all times, however, you will soon find yourself in the enviable position of being the foreman of choice.

LOSS OF RESPECT

Earning respect is like earning credibility. It does not come from the title on your business card or the fact that you drive a company truck. There will always be those foremen who believe that they are due the respect of their peers simply because they have been given a business card with their name on it, but nothing could be further from the truth. Success will be yours only if the people who work for you hold you, your work, and your leadership skills in high esteem.

Also like credibility, respect is earned through action, not words. As a foreman you are asking your crew to be efficient and productive. If they don't see you approaching your job with the same intent, your respect as a leader will come into question and, ultimately, disappear.

The saying is old, but still holds true: you have to lead by example. The better example you set for your crew, the more respect they will have for you and the harder they will work for you.

LOSING THE JOB

It should be pretty obvious that if you don't do a good job, you probably won't have a job for long. But the connection between poor planning and the loss of a job may be harder to see.

Let's say your lack of planning has led to a number of less than satisfactory projects and your company is not happy with your results. If the company wants to keep you on, they will probably offer you training first. If this effort fails, they'll have no choice other than to demote you from your position as foreman or to let you go altogether. The hard reality is that most foremen in the construction industry do not get training and do not get demoted; instead they are simply let go. Learning how to plan keeps you and your career in the best shape for as long as you want it.

FINAL THOUGHTS

Chapter 7 is titled "Planning: Your Top Priority." Don't lose sight of the fact that every aspect of being successful starts with a well-laid plan. If this weren't the case, then anyone could show up to a job site and do your job. We all know that's not possible, and that it would be both inefficient and ineffective. It's also clear that a project's fighting chance at maximum success rides on your shoulders and hinges on your dedication to good planning.

Chapter 10

Planning Challenges

Inherent to any job, or anything you want to do well, are challenges that need to be overcome if you want to be successful. The construction industry is no different. Therefore, it may be troubling to learn that many of the challenges you'll face as a foreman in this industry will be things you were never taught in your apprenticeship and that were never talked about by the foremen you worked for in the past. The best foremen and leaders know what these challenges are and know how to head them off at the pass. It is up to you to learn what they know.

Since no one is totally immune to these challenges, it is how you deal with them that makes the difference. I know because I am constantly working on my own ability to keep the challenges that come up from becoming too much of a distraction or allowing them to affect the success of the projects I run. Some of the challenges mentioned here will apply to you; some may not. Everyone is different. For those that do strike a chord in you, it remains up to you, and you alone, to be aware of their existence and do something about how you handle them. At the end of any project, whether it turns out well or not so well, you are the only one who will know if you have done everything in your power to ensure a successful outcome.

INABILITY TO FOCUS

It's not unusual for a foreman to become overwhelmed by the many tasks and responsibilities on his plate at any one time. When this happens, he may lose his ability to plan and stay organized. Even worse, he may find that his brain shifts to overload and becomes almost paralyzed. With so many things running around in a foreman's head all at once, it's no wonder that he can lose the ability to focus on one task at a time to its completion.

Let me just say that it is normal for this to happen occasionally to the best of us. But if you let it consume you, your effectiveness as a leader will be compromised. If you are a first-time foreman, you already know what it's like to feel overwhelmed by the job. Your responsibilities have increased exponentially, most of them responsibilities you never had to consider before. As a consequence, you constantly feel that you can't possibly get everything done that needs to be done.

The good news is that all you have to do is add a few new tools to your tool belt. The following suggestions and guidelines should help.

1. *Do one thing at a time*. Sounds simple, right? But all of us tend to forget that we can only do one thing at a time—that is, if we expect to do it well. My experience with

self-proclaimed "multi-taskers" has only solidified my belief that it's best to tackle the planning and solving of problems one at a time. Many of us believe that we can drive and text someone at the same time, for example, but the number of accidents on the road proves otherwise.

For most of us, multi-tasking only ends up minimizing the effort that we put into each task, ultimately leaving a lot to be desired in the results department. I admit that to the naked eye multi-tasking can appear pretty impressive—carrying on two phone calls, writing an email, and gesturing to someone to take out the trash all at the same time. But the reality is that the person on the other end of the phone likely feels slighted, the email probably has errors that will have to be corrected later on, and the gesture to take out the trash probably caused the person on the receiving end to want to throw it at your head—if he even knew what you were telling him to do.

In fact, I've heard that studies have shown that the brain is literally only capable of doing one thing at a time. That means we just *think* we're doing a number of things at once. So, if we're really only going back and forth among different tasks quickly, it's extremely likely we're doing none of them as well as we think we are. I personally have never been and have never known a truly proficient multi-tasker.

With all that said, being a foreman often forces you to respond to multiple tasks, seemingly at the same time. I have found that the difference lies in the element of focus, where the primary focus should always be on the plan. That means that making your plan requires your full, undivided attention when you are creating it. If the task at hand gets your full focus you will likely avoid making serious project missteps that can lead to other planning errors, re-work, and omissions during installation.

It's easy to say you need "undivided attention," but finding that time is something else again. I know it's not easy, especially when you have people demanding your time to get their own jobs done. That's why your approach needs to be one of assigning yourself the time just as you would your crewmembers.

The best times to take a few minutes where you will be less likely to be disturbed and less likely to be distracted are very early or very late in the day. At other times you will undoubtedly find yourself busy working out all the different issues that come up with your crew.

2. *Make a list.* I know we've discussed lists before. But lists provide an excellent way to focus your attention and your energy when you need it the most. What do you need to get? What do you need to do? Who do you have to talk to? All these things should end up on your list to be handled during the time you've set aside at the beginning or end of your day.

The reality is that you may never find yourself at the true end of your list because it will continue to grow even as you check off tasks that you are accomplishing. That's the nature of the job. But if you keep a master list that is always being revised based on new and completed tasks from your crew and other trades, you will always feel you have things under control.

You can keep your master list on your computer, digital device, or on a pad of paper in your trailer, but the goal is to never be without a way to record the new issues that crop up while you are out walking the job site. A small notebook that fits in your pocket is a great solution, and the items you mark down can easily be transferred to your master list when you get back to the trailer. In fact, just the act of transferring the information at the end of the day can help to reorganize your thinking and refocus your energy for future planning purposes.

3. *Recording devices.* Another option I sometimes use myself is to keep notes on a digital recorder. Nowadays digital recorders are smaller than cell phones and you can keep them with you at all times. Something comes up? Leave yourself a reminder. It's easy to turn on your recorder and talk for a minute when you're walking away from a conversation and while the thought is still fresh in your mind. Not only are you more likely to finish your thoughts without being interrupted, but you won't have to stop to write it all down. And since these recorders usually date- and time-stamp your notes, you don't have to worry about those specifics either. Just say it and forget it—until the end of the day or the next morning.

    Another plus for the recorder is that you can take it into your coordination meetings, something that allows you to focus on the meeting rather than on taking notes. Because most recorders come with software you can then transfer anything you record onto the hard drive of your computer.

THE SUPERMAN COMPLEX

I've always found it a little funny that some of the same foremen who carry around a digital camera to document the work that *has been* done don't take the care to document what still *needs* to be done. Foremen like this tend to fall into the same category as those who don't write things down because they think it's "a big waste of time."

First of all, unless you're Superman, keeping everything that happens on a job site in your head without forgetting any of it—or even half of it—is an unlikely prospect. If you think you can you're only fooling yourself. Yes, everyone is different, but no one is without limitations—even Superman. I have worked for and alongside people through the years who don't write anything down. It probably won't come as a surprise that they are the same ones who consistently drop the ball. They might forget to order material their crew needs for the next day or about a commitment they made to their customer. Either way, forgetting brings the kind of results you don't want.

I have often tried to figure out the reasoning behind the unwillingness to keep notes and lists, but have come up empty. Can we chalk it up to laziness? Do these people truly believe they don't need to write things down because their memories are so superior? I don't know. But if you are one of them and constantly in a reactionary mode because of it, you are doing a disservice to your crew, your company, your customer, and, most of all, yourself. Each time you are held accountable but do not come through, you lose another small piece of your credibility. It may not seem like a big deal at the time, but over the long run it adds up.

DEALING WITH INTERRUPTIONS

Interruptions are as unavoidable as hard hats in the construction business. That's why we need ways to constantly remind us how to stay on task. For example, if you get called away from the task at hand while you're in the process of planning and detailing, grab a sticky note and jot down exactly where you left off, as well the thoughts you were having when you were interrupted. I am always amazed, no matter how engrossed I am in what I'm doing, how easy it is to lose track of where I was. If the task goes untouched until the next day, there's an even greater chance that some of my thoughts will have erased themselves forever. You can never hurt yourself by making too many notes, and you just might save your sanity in the process.

TIME *MIS*MANAGEMENT

Ever suggest that someone take a time management class? If you did, I'll bet you got this response: "Who me? I don't have the time!" There will be plenty of people who read this section who will take the suggestions personally or brush them off because they feel they don't have the time to think about them, let alone apply them. If this is the case and you find they truly don't apply to you, then let me congratulate you on being the only human capable of having total control over his mind and body. You could write a book called *The Zen of Foremanship*—and if you did, I'd be the first to buy it. But the rest of us need all the help we can get.

To be frank, and at the risk of alienating some of my readers, I did not write this book for those people who feel they are already doing the best they are capable of doing or those who want to make excuses and blame others for their lack of success. I wrote it for those of you who want to be great leaders, who won't stop at good enough. If this sounds like you, and you're willing to look, you'll probably find a habit or two mentioned below that you'd like to eliminate from your life. It is up to you to decide to make that change or to continue to do things the way you have always done.

"HANG ON A MINUTE..."

Let's start with the habit of using your cell phone for personal calls while you're at work. The world has changed! With the advent of the cell phone, we have all become addicted to the ability to call anyone at any time—or to take calls from anyone all the time. The problem starts when the addiction encroaches on our time at work. Sure, we all have business and personal issues outside of the job, and occasionally they may require our attention with a phone call in the middle of the day. But we also have to be honest that most of the calls we get are not urgent, or even super important. So that leaves us with time spent on the phone that could be spent on other more pressing job-related concerns.

Plenty of foremen are heard to argue that because they frequently put in more time than they are getting paid for they have earned that time. Let's assume this is the case. After all, in all fairness, it probably *is* true that they are putting in at least some extra time. The snag comes because most often these are the same foremen who haven't put in the necessary time for planning and, hence, aren't running an efficient job. The upshot is this: Even if you have put in more time, you still need to maximize the time you spend at work, perhaps for the express purchase of doing some extra planning! And every call you take contributes to your ability to be distracted from the task at hand.

On-the-job Training: On the Job

A contractor comes to your house to fix a plumbing (or electrical or roof) problem. This contractor gets paid by the hour. Suddenly, instead of finding him in the bathroom (or at the breaker box or on the roof) you see him standing out by his truck talking on his cell phone. Half an hour later when he's still there you begin to wonder if his conversation could possibly be related to this job he is supposedly there to do for *you.*

Would you pay this contractor for the time he spent on his cell phone? There's no way. I'll bet you wouldn't hesitate to let him know that you intended to pay him only for the time he actually worked on your project...and I'll bet you wouldn't budge an inch from that position.

How is it any different, then, when you are a foreman who is working for a contractor who pays you by the hour? Admittedly, there is one big difference in that you probably fill out your own time card, so if you're spending too much time on the phone no one will know. I know I've never met a foreman who docked himself at the end of the week for the time he spent on personal phone calls. But next time you hear the phone ring, do yourself a favor and think about what you've just read.

There's another problem with taking and making lots of calls during work hours. It refers back to what we discussed earlier about asking your crew to do something that you aren't willing to do yourself. It's perfectly reasonable to expect your employees to refrain from using their personal cell phones except during breaks, lunch, or for an absolute emergency. But if you don't hold yourself to the same standard, lack of awareness on your part will breed contempt.

I think we all harbor a certain sense of entitlement based on the fact that we put in extra time that we don't see reflected in the paycheck. The question is not whether you *are* entitled, however. It's whether your crew understands, too. And I can guarantee they do not. They will not see the extra time you're putting in because they come to work after you arrive and probably go home before you do most of the time. Don't let them see you on the phone if you want them to keep theirs in their pockets.

SURFING THE WEB

Another way to mismanage time is to be indiscriminate about the time you spend surfing the Internet. Time slips away faster online than in almost any other activity. Having a computer and Internet access so you can research information that is job-related and to have the ability to send and receive email is a great advantage on any project. But we all know how easy it is to get sidetracked. Before you know it, a chunk of time has virtually disappeared without even blinking. Working as a journeyman and a foreman, I've come across many situations where I've walked into the foreman's trailer to find him looking up interests of a personal nature. It is not for me to judge what foremen do with their free time, but since time at work isn't free...well, you do the math.

IT'S PERSONAL...

There's not too much to say about personal conversations other than they are simply that: personal. If you are spending an excessive amount of time communicating on a personal level with your crewmembers or members of other trades, it's time to take note. I don't know anybody who isn't guilty of this at one time or another, and I do believe that in order to get to know each crewmember and build morale and trust with each one, you have to take some time to get to know them. But I believe the best policy is to do it in such a way where you're not spending large amounts of time that take away from what you both really need to be doing. You know better than anyone that anytime you slow down the production of someone on your crew, that time has to be made up somewhere else by someone else. Maybe even you.

BURNED OUT

Do you feel burned out? Are you one of those foremen who seem ready to give up at the end of the day or end of the week? Do you know a foreman like this—someone who wanders the job with no particular reason in mind other than getting out of their trailer and avoiding work?

Don't get me wrong. I believe it's important for the foreman to walk the job. I also think it's advantageous to take a break when you have been going hard at planning and detailing for a few hours straight. But we both know I'm not talking about that.

I'm talking about coasting across the finish line when the race isn't yet over.

Sure, I get it. It's human nature. Especially when you've had a difficult and stressful week. But if you find yourself "wandering" on a regular basis while you still have a big workload to finish, then you aren't facing the fact that you're on a dangerous trajectory. Yes, it takes discipline, perhaps to be more focused early in the day or to take a shorter lunch hour and finish up some things that have slipped away.

The point is that if you let yourself off the hook too often you'll be correct when you say you don't have enough time to get all your work done. On the flip side, pushing through burn-out is a sure sign of a true professional and a successful foreman.

FINAL THOUGHTS

These are all legitimate, common ways in which we can mismanage our time. It's impossible to avoid all of them all of the time, but being aware of the pitfalls they pose can save you from that slippery slope of denial.

If you're one of the ones who believe they've earned the right to use their time at work the way they want...well, I don't mean to be harsh, but save it. Great leaders don't make excuses; they just get the job done.

Chapter 11

Planning in Phases

It is the nature of a plan that we only really know if it is solid once it's been executed and has proven to be successful. With that said, after executing enough successful plans and projects, I can say without hesitation that solid plans are best achieved through the use of a four-phase process.

There are many aspects of putting together a great plan, but identifying and carrying out the following four phases will ensure your plan will function well and to completion. Note that no one part is any more important than any other, and that if you remove any one of these stages from the process you will likely end up with a plan that is subpar.

PHASE 1: DETAILING

Detailing is the critical first step of the planning process. It means removing as much of the guesswork as possible from every new task you assign your crew. The goal is to eliminate as many questions as possible before the work begins, such as dimensions, materials to be used, the approach, and so on. Don't forget that compared to your knowledge of the prints, specifications, and the project as a whole, your crew's will always be limited. If you expect them to be as productive as possible, it is your responsibility to prepare all the information, materials, and tools they need before the inception of the project or task.

Detailing also includes dissecting every part of your prints to determine the very best way possible to make your installation. During this process you're bound to come across discrepancies, such as conflicts with other trades, incomplete information, and questions about an installation, or you may need an interpretation from an architect or engineer explaining his intent.

It helps to write these things down!

There is nothing worse than getting to a point in the project before you realize that you don't have all of the information needed to complete your installation. You'll be even more frustrated if it was something you'd noticed months earlier, but had forgotten to pursue.

GETTING TO THE BOTTOM OF IT

Unfortunately, it's not always possible to get immediately to the bottom of issues or questions. A quick answer is not always available. When you write a request for information (RFI) to the architects or engineers, for example, it can take weeks to get an answer. Sometimes they can answer a question right off of the top of their heads, but other times they will have to talk to the customer or another architect or engineer who helped during the design process.

DETAILED DOCUMENTING

Once you've gotten the information you need, it is vital to take your answers and document them in such a way that anyone looking for them can find them. Every set of prints in the field your crew references needs to be updated with the latest information and revisions.

If crewmembers are left in the dark, the installation will suffer from errors and valuable time and money will be lost.

PLAYING NICELY WITH OTHERS

Another part of detailing requires you to work with the other trades on your project. Working well alongside other trades helps you eliminate the chance of having to lay something out numerous times, and being a team player who is willing to help the other trades be efficient and productive increases your credibility and the respect from other foremen and the rest of the crew. Don't wait for the other trades to come to you for coordination and detailing questions. Be proactive—especially if no one else is. You want to be the one driving the job whenever possible.

> **If you wait for someone else to take the lead, you'll end up doing things their way. Most of the time their way won't be what's best for you and your company.**

DETAILING DOWN THE LINE

As with planning, detailing should start the very first day and continue throughout the project. Some part of every day needs to be set aside to detail some specific future part of the job. Every day you do not plan and detail, your crew gets one step closer to catching you without a good plan in place.

Detailing is best done as far ahead of the time you anticipate needing it as possible. This can really make a difference when the job is in full swing and you're getting pulled in what feels like a million different directions. If slower times exist, they will be at the beginning of the project. Don't let yourself off the hook with the attitude that the rest will take care of itself. Believe me, it won't. These slower times are by far the best times to work on planning and detailing, before they are gone for good. Realistically, they may be the only time when you can study, focus without being interrupted, and stay on task.

ASKING FOR HELP

Once a project ramps up to full speed it gets harder and harder to plan and detail. If at any point it becomes too much too handle, you as the foreman have to either ask for help or find a way to get it done. Again, don't wait until it's too late. Letting the work pile up, knowing you can't complete all of it, only sets you and the project up for failure. Communicate with your supervisor as soon as you recognize that you need help, before you find yourself so buried that you can't recover and while it can still have a positive impact on the outcome of the job. Don't forget that your project manager may be able to offer some support in the form of more manpower or help you prioritize what needs to be done to get through the big push.

PHASE 2: TOOLS AND MATERIAL REQUISITION

Determining the tools and material you'll need to have on site throughout the many phases of your project is the natural next step of your planning and detailing process.

The key is to make your requisitions list detailed enough to cover all the material quantities and all the tools that you will need. It is absolutely crucial that you have these things on site *before* your crew needs them. Having layout and no tools or tools and no material will put a halt to your installation before you can say *Shoot, why didn't I make a list?*

None of these items is more important than any other. The lack of even one—layout, material, or tools—and your crew will be at a stand still. It's impossible to think of every single thing you'll require for an entire project, but it should be perfectly doable to have everything you need for the tasks in the works over the next few weeks.

ORDERING

A couple of simple tips for ordering material will save you time and money:

1. *Don't under-order commonly used inexpensive items.* If you know you're going to need 5,000 bolts throughout the length of a project, don't order them 200 at a time. Your crew could easily burn those up in a day. The next thing you know, they're standing around and you're spending valuable time running around trying to borrow some from another trade. Again, there's no getting back the amount of labor that stands to be wasted when your crew doesn't have what they need. It's true that you need to be mindful of the materials you buy and always try to keep waste at a minimum, but a good foreman recognizes that wasted labor can add up to much bigger numbers than having a box of bolts left over at the end of a project.

2. *Look for commonly available discounts on material that you buy in larger quantities.* If you have the room to store some larger quantities of material you can save your project money.

3. *Lock it up!* Are you concerned that the more material you have the more other trades are going to help themselves to it? If so, lock it up. The potential that your material might be taken is not a good enough excuse for ordering such small quantities that your crew will be stuck without something it needs. It's a cheap and easy solution to get gang boxes and give everyone on your crew a key. Just make sure that you communicate to your crew that you want it locked 24/7. Without exception.

4. *Speciality tools.* There will always be certain tools and material that won't be available simply by running down

to the supply house and picking them up off the shelf. As soon as you identify those items, put together a schedule and a plan how to get those items on site. There's nothing worse than having your crew ready and willing only to discover that the speciality tool you need will be unavailable for another week.

Another side affect of not having what your crew needs is that you may be unable to complete the work you are on the schedule to do. When this happens you put every trade that follows you in a tough position to get their work done on time. These are all indications to rethink your process.

To be honest, I'd have lost my mind a long time ago if I'd been a contractor watching the amount of wasted labor I've witnessed over the last 20 years. Construction is unique in that the crew is very rarely within eyesight of the foreman. For this reason, he can be oblivious to the hours thrown away when the crew cannot find what they need to complete their work. Unless someone on the crew speaks up the foreman may never know. I see it as the foreman's responsibility to keep this kind of waste from happening.

On-the-Job Training: Figuring Out the Burn Rate

When you are the foreman, whatever trade you're in, in order to truly understand the consequences of wasted labor you need to know what your employees' actual "burn rate" is per hour. For our purposes, we'll look at the amount each individual makes per hour and then add in all the benefits they receive beyond that hourly wage. If you don't know what these benefit packages include and how much they're worth, ask your company. Someone in human resources will always know exactly how much each person costs the company for every hour of work.

Then take the number for the individual's hourly total wage and then divide it by 60 minutes. This will let you assign a dollar value to the amount that employee racks up in the red column every time he spends 20 to 30 minutes searching for a tool or material he should have had readily available to him.

You can justify the sharing of some expensive specialty tools, but not those like extension cords, socket sets, or ladders. Tools like these are so inexpensive in relation to wasted labor that an employee should never have to go far to find one of them.

5. *On-site deliveries.* Same-day deliveries and heavy competition among supply houses has changed the way we do business, particularly in larger market areas. When suppliers are willing to jump through hoops to get your order it's easy to become a little complacent (that is, lazy) because you get used to assuming that you can always get what you want with the snap of your fingers.

   If you are in a location that does not have access to these services, you may be more prone to plan ahead. But for those with almost unlimited access to goods and services, access can also lead to poor planning. The foreman who never plans more than a day or two—or even an hour or two!—ahead is just waiting for the axe to fall. You may find this hard to believe, but I have watched foremen call a taxi service, have the driver go to the supply house to pick up the material ordered at the very last minute, and then have the taxi driver deliver the material to the job site. In my view this is the epitome of poor planning, a poor solution to a self-imposed crisis, and in opposition to the most basic responsibilities of the foreman: to manage the most efficient and productive project possible.

Here is how such a maneuver hurts the bottom line.

First of all, if your standard mode of operation has you constantly about to run out of material, at some point your crew will be out of what they need. Obvious, but true. So it should be just as obvious why habitually ordering only for the next day or two ahead will make and keep your project perpetually inefficient. Second, can you imagine having to explain to your company why they're paying for a taxi service? There is no possible explanation for your actions that will have them see your management abilities in a positive light.

Third, every time a delivery comes to your site someone on your crew has to stop what he is doing to sign for it and then unload the truck. Then the material has to be taken to your on-site storage area to be stocked. If you only had a delivery once or twice a week, one that included an entire week's worth of material, just think about how much more efficient and effective your project would be.

Fourth, when deliveries flood in without planned scheduling crewmembers are much more likely to take what they need and push the rest aside. Many of these materials will then get lost in all the activity, never to be found again.

Fifth, if you have ordered material for three different crewmembers and two of them don't even know the material has arrived, they could end up waiting a lot longer than they should. You know what happens next: you end up having to re-order what you know you already have somewhere but can't find to keep the job moving forward.

Finally, every job site is different in terms if how deliveries are handled. Some sites assign delivery times to avoid bottlenecks when multiple trucks show up at the same time. Sometimes it can be logistically challenging to get your material and tools through the site to where they are needed. Some deliveries require forklifts or cranes to be unloaded, and need even more specialized attention and planning. Nobody likes to have a delivery show up with no way of getting the items off the truck.

IT'S WORTH THE TROUBLE

Designing your time on the job to order your material more than a day or two in advance turns out to be much less trouble than doing otherwise. Stop and think about the needs of your crew, what they are doing, and what they will be doing down the line. You are the one providing the direction. It's up to you to put a system in place for getting the material and making sure it gets to where it needs to be. On larger projects with multiple foremen and crews spread throughout the site, the individual decisions made by each foreman matter all that much more.

PHASE 3: MANPOWER

Now that you've scheduled and handled all the parts related to tools and materials, it's time to look at your crew. How big a crew will you need? When will you need to ramp up or down? A well-done detailed plan provides an excellent guide for building an accurate manpower chart.

CHARTING YOUR MANPOWER

Once you have built your chart, discuss your manpower needs with your supervisor, who can then build his own schedule to ensure you get the help you need when you need it. Keep in mind that your supervisor has probably already built his own manpower chart during the design or estimating process. This means you'll both need to be in agreement as to when you will ramp up and when you will ramp down. Even though you have spent a lot of time planning and building your chart, don't make the mistake of thinking that it's etched in stone. Just like the rest of your plan, it is a necessary reference tool that will continue to be a work in progress.

If instead of having a plan you make the mistake of adding people whenever you think you need them, you will never know when you have crossed the line into putting the project's success in jeopardy.

SIZING UP YOUR MANPOWER

You've heard me say it before, but there is no more important message in this book:

Labor hours that get wasted will cost your project more money, and at a faster rate, than anything else.

That's why, as foreman, it's up to you (and your supervisor) to make sure the crew is always the right size for the job. As soon as you reach a point in the project where you feel you have too large a crew for the remaining amount of work, it's time to slim down your crew. The hours you save may be needed later in the project; if they aren't, they'll be added to the profits of your project at the end.

The trap of keeping too many people on your crew as things start to slow down is a common one. It is every foreman's fear that as soon as he starts to send part of his crew away he'll suddenly be buried and unable to keep up. Fight these thoughts when you know the time is right to cut back! Temporary help is always available to bring back on site for a short time if absolutely necessary. What you can't get back are labor hours that have been wasted or spent inefficiently.

On-the-Job Training: Too Many Crew

You're the foreman on a project. You're waiting impatiently for another trade to finish its part of an installation. For this reason, you don't have enough work to keep your entire crew busy and productive. Because you are fearful that you'll lose them, you choose to find busy work for some of them instead of sending them away.

What happens? Valuable labor hours are burned up. Energy, time, and money are wasted.

Too many people on your crew can damage your efficiency.

It's easy to lose sight of the bigger picture when this happens, and to imagine that it will be helpful to have your oversized crew spend this time finishing all of the small incidental tasks that have been sitting on your list of things to complete...things like finish work, labeling, and so on. But this is a stop-gap measure that rarely works. At some point, if you continue to use a large crew to complete these smaller tasks you will run out of work for the entire crew. As much as these things need to be done, they generally can be accomplished at the tail end of the job as you and a small crew finish up.

This is not to say that it's good to wait until the last minute, but rather to trim your crew while you wait for the other trade to finish its installation and have a small crew working on your list of smaller projects in the meantime.

CUTTING BACK TOO SOON

We've talked about the problems that arise with having too much crew for too long. But there's also a concern when you cut back your crew too soon. It's all about finding the middle ground and knowing how to maintain the equilibrium.

There are always those over-aggressive foremen and project managers who try to increase their profits by cutting a crew back a little too early. The downside of this maneuver is it can put you in the position of missing schedules and scrambling to complete tasks. It might seem like a good idea at the time because you'll have lessened the labor hours spent, but without carefully factoring every possibility, your decision could come back to bite you. Consider the three following scenarios.

On-the-Job Training: Cutting Back

One, you've cut back your crew too early. Soon you're falling behind schedule. You don't know what to do.

Two, you've cut back your crew too early. Soon you fall behind schedule. You crack the whip on the small crew you have left, but they can only do what they can do. You end up coming across as the foreman with the unreasonable expectations. You push the crew even harder. Soon they start to feel resentful that you cut the rest of the crew back and are now demanding them to work even harder than they were before. Your decision has begun to backfire.

Three, you've cut back your crew too early and have fallen behind schedule. You're cracking the whip on the small crew you have left, but now they see you as the foreman with the unreasonable expectations and resent your demands. Then one of your tasks hits a snag and prevents you from moving

> on to other tasks on the schedule that need attention. The crew feels the added stress. So do you.

Ultimately, your goal is to meet your schedules, partly so the other trades who follow you won't have to scramble to make their schedules. Otherwise dissention between you and the other trades' foremen will be the natural, unwelcome, outcome.

PHASE 4: COORDINATION

Working with all the other trades on your project is a multidimensional process. Once you have a plan, recognize that it does not stand on its own and that working with the other trades to make sure that your plan works for them, too, is part of this mechanism. They will also be planning and organizing what they need to build their portion of the project. Working together to coordinate your plan with theirs allows for the opportunity to identify potential conflicts, making them easier to remedy prior to the onset of installations.

FORGING PARTNERSHIPS

Nobody likes a job-site bully! Working with other trades means maintaining partnerships, not establishing a dictatorship. A bully who thinks his trade should take priority and that everyone else should work around him creates dissention and discomfort on the site, whereas finding the common goal only improves everyone's chances for a profitable outcome.

On projects where the various trades don't work well together, making a profit becomes difficult if not impossible. It becomes a battle to see who can get his work done first. This, in turn, causes stress, tension, and resentment for all. And once the finger pointing starts, I can promise you that climbing back up to where you began will not be easy.

LEADING

Even though a foreman's number-one goal at this point is coordination, don't mistake coordination with not taking a lead position.

Being a leader is always of primary importance in achieving your objectives. For example, as the schedule is formed make sure that your input is taken into consideration. If it is not, you will constantly be playing catch-up and you'll be at a disadvantage, reacting to the actions of the other trades. If you let other trades dictate how you proceed, you'll end up in a permanent reactionary mode. Essentially, you'll have given the other trades the right to always put their interests ahead of yours. Bear in mind that the other foreman are responsible only to *their* companies and to the success of *their* portion of the project, so it is up to you to make sure that the plan is coordinated together, with *everyone's* input.

COMPANY COORDINATION

Communication is the key to adept and successful coordination efforts. First, you will need things from your own company, such as manpower, tools, and material delivery. When you're out on a job site and your supervisor or support staff is at another location, unless you communicate your needs it will be impossible for them to know what they can do to help you out.

Good communication means giving the home office as much notice as you can so they won't be blindsided every time you call. Most supervisors and support staff are responsible for many different projects that are running simultaneously, so it may not always be easy for them to drop everything to try and help you out. If you become the foreman who cries wolf—who is always calling up at the last minute with an "emergency"—you'll not only lose credibility with your supervisor, but it's likely you won't get the help when you really do have a situation that warrants it.

My advice? Don't wait to change your communication methods until your supervisor has realized that the reason you constantly have your back against the wall is because of your lack of planning and coordination.

Chapter 12

Planning and Safety

This section on planning wouldn't be complete without a discussion about how good planning results in a safer work environment. Construction work is, by nature, a physically demanding and dangerous vocation. It takes everyone, starting from the top on down, to do his part to make sure that injuries and accidents are avoided at all cost.

ACCOMPLISHING THE TASK SAFELY

Detailing your plans for each task does not stop with scheduling crews, tools, and material. Just as important is the attention you pay to how you intend to accomplish every single task safely. It may be as simple as making sure that your crew always wears their hard hats or requiring your crew to be in safety harnesses and tied off when they are working at the leading edge of a building. No matter how big or small, how obviously dangerous or seemingly secure, good safety practices cannot be assumed or overlooked.

It is always *your* responsibility as the foreman to make sure that your crew have whatever they need to remain safe and injury-free whenever and wherever they need it. They are relying on you to provide this equipment, just as they rely on you to provide the tools, material, and information they are not expected to go out and get on their own. If you want to guarantee your crew is doing everything in its power to be safe, then you have to make it known that you will not tolerate anything less. How? By providing what they need, setting a good example, and communicating your expectations.

CONSISTENT SAFETY

When it comes to safety, how your crew perceives the legitimacy of the statements you make determines how they proceed when met with a difficult situation. Their reaction will be predetermined by your consistency; that is, what you have said and done in the past. There are plenty of foremen who give pretty convincing speeches at safety meetings about how important safety is. I know because I've heard them. I've also seen them minutes or hours later do something themselves, or ask someone else to do something, that is unsafe or even dangerous. I call this "talking out the side of your neck." Unfortunately, this trend runs rampant in the construction industry.

It is in the nature of human beings to consciously or subconsciously size each other up. It's no different for your crew and coworkers, who will determine in their own minds if we are honest, if we have integrity. If we consistently fall short of the image we portray, we can expect to lose any loyalty, respect, and credibility that we may once have had.

Allowing unsafe practices or condoning poor attitudes toward safety is just as irresponsible as having the incorrect equipment. Either way you're inviting disaster. I've watched dangerous work continue because someone chooses not to go find the needed equipment because it will slow down production. I've watched dangerous work continue because the work site is so strewn with tools and materials that the safety equipment is impossible to locate in all the mess. Without order and protocol for organizing and storing the safety equipment it will not be available when it is needed. Without it you put yourself, your crew, your project, and your company at risk.

SAFE TALK

Sometimes lack of communication affects safety as well. If an individual doesn't feel comfortable asking you, the foreman, for the equipment he needs, that's a problem. Put yourself in the position of your employee. Ask yourself why someone would risk getting hurt or hurting someone else for the sake of production—or for the sake of not bothering you.

On the other hand, if your employee is simply slack when it comes to safety, it could be because he doesn't feel there will be any real consequences if his foreman were to see him working in unsafe conditions. If this is the case, it falls on you to make it very clear what you expect of each employee—to put safety first—while making sure each employee understands that no one will ever be penalized for doing things the right way.

RISKY BEHAVIOR

You might be surprised to learn that a lot of people take unnecessary risks because they actually think they are doing the foreman a favor by "taking care of business" in a timely manner. Certainly these are people who don't realize the position they are putting you in if they were to get hurt. Remember, the first person your company or accident investigator will turn to if an accident occurs on your job site will be *you*. And when they do, you had better have some good answers for them.

Probably the most powerful reason for an individual's taking a risk that jeopardizes safety is his fear that he will lose production time if he takes the time he needs to do his task correctly *and* safely. If asked, this individual will probably say that taking that time will somehow be counted against him. In my experience, this is the explanation most often given for making a person make the judgment call to do something in an unsafe way.

When you think about it, it shouldn't be that hard to stifle this way of thinking. All you need to do is communicate clearly and often to your entire crew that safety comes first. Show your crew you mean what you say by taking any safety concern they bring to you seriously. One roll of the eyes or a discount of their concern is all it takes to discourage them from talking to you in the future...and encourage them to think less of you and your credibility.

On-the-Job Training: The Measuring Stick

The construction industry has always been a competitive work environment and production is the measuring stick. The fact that you are reading this book proves that you understand that being a better foreman increases production. So when it comes to cutbacks and layoffs, every employee knows that it is the highest skilled and most productive workers that will be kept on longest.

People's livelihoods depend on their ability to stay on the payroll. If your crew is always worried about slowing down their personal production to incorporate safety measures, why would they take these measures to heart?

Answer: They wouldn't. That's why it's up to you to set the bar, and set it high.

RISK AND REPUTATION

There's no way to write a book about the construction industry without addressing its reputation for employing a bunch of fearless roughnecks who hang off the side of skyscrapers by their belt loops without a care in the world. Unfortunately, that kind of macho attitude of indestructibility is what gets people hurt. Any individual who is cavalier in his approach to safety or who has a misconception about what is being asked of him but doesn't want to admit it is much more likely to make bad decisions. There are too many individuals who participate in unsafe practices out of fear of being ridiculed by their coworkers—or foremen. Ridicule, especially around safety, is detrimental to a positive work environment.

Nobody on your crew wants to be seen by his peers as the weakest link or a whiner. This is why communicating your expectations to your entire crew is so vital to their ongoing safety. You need to convince them that you will do your best to look out for them, but that they are responsible for taking care of each other when you are not around. For those individuals who do not want to participate in a safe work environment, it's your job to have a one-on-one conversation with them and let them know there will be consequences following any insubordinate actions.

COMMON EXCUSES

I'll bet if we looked at statistics of those individuals who have been injured or died while working on a construction site we'd find the reasons cited above as the answer to why things hadn't gotten done the right way. I'll also bet if you were to talk to the foremen of those injured or killed workers who were responsible for their safety, they'd say that they wished they had done something more to convince their crew that safety was their number-one priority. Poor decisions leading to serious injury or death cannot help but haunt everyone involved for the rest of their lives.

It's a painful reality, then, to face the fact that many foremen believe there is so much to do already that safety is just one more thing that demands their already thin attention. To argue this point borders on the irrelevant, however, because if you and your crew don't work safe, there is a good chance you'll find yourself without a job, and possibly in a courtroom defending your negligence regarding an accident on your job site.

There are far-reaching consequences for the foreman who is negligent or chooses to look the other way when it comes to safety. If you allow yourself to ignore your responsibility to safety, you are taking a big personal risk.

GUILT STICKS

First, don't underestimate the guilt you'll feel if someone is injured or killed on your watch. Guilt stays with you 24 hours a day, reminding you of your part in whatever has occurred. You can't get away from it, and for the rest of your life you will be asking yourself, *What if?* There isn't anyone I know who wouldn't be devastated by having an accident happen because he did not make absolutely clear what he expected from his crew or because he didn't provide the proper equipment.

Your employees are just as important to their friends and families as you are to yours. Every single person on your crew deserves to go home every night the same way he arrived in the morning. Don't let a small inconvenience or a decrease in production cause you to make a decision that you will regret for the rest of your life.

JOB LOSS

Taking undue safety risks can easily lead to your losing your job. Your company's insurance rates are largely based on its safety record and the amount of recordable injuries that occur over a measured period of time. If your company believes that as a foreman you are a liability and your track record warrants action they will have no choice but to demote you or let you go. It's simply the way the business works. Sure, you can find another job, but is it worth it?

LITIGATION

Being party to unsafe practices also leads many foremen into court. You could find yourself called as a witness, or even worse as a defendant in the litigation process. Death and injury on a construction site always means someone will be looking to be compensated for what was lost. For an injured employee it might "only" be wages for lost time and medical expenses. If the injury causes the employee to be permanently disabled then the stakes are much higher, possibly compensating him for a lifetime of lost wages. When a family loses a loved one there is only one type of compensation possible and that's monetary.

If you are the foreman responsible when an individual gets hurt or dies, you will be front and center for as long as the litigation continues. If it can be proven there was gross negligence on your part and that the accident could have been avoided, it might also lead to your incarceration.

These words are not meant to scare you. They are meant to project the need for safety for you and your crew and to encourage you to think about the consequences and do what's right on the job. On every job.

Chapter 13

Executing Your Plan

It's time! All your hard work detailing and planning is now coming to fruition. Its value is obvious in your smoothly running project, which flows with a nice constant rhythm and has a good feeling of timing and order. You don't find yourself flying by the seat of your pants all of the time and you aren't constantly caught unprepared. Because you've taken the right approach, you feel confident handling any problems or modifications that come your way.

Feels good, right? Absolutely. But execution of your plan will always remain an ongoing challenge. All construction projects have their own unique demands. The key is to do your best to form an educated and informed strategy for approaching the problems that may occur. That way you can minimize surprises and have the peace of mind that comes with knowing that you'll always have a contingency plan.

SETTING PRIORITIES

As you direct your crew throughout the project, always attempt to complete your highest priority tasks first to keep you ahead of schedule and avoid getting backed into a corner. No matter how long or short your list of tasks, take the time to *number them in order of priority*. Update your list frequently. If your crew is currently completing tasks that could be done at a later time, you may be inadvertently eliminating part of the contingency plan you put in place for when the job slow downs or hits a snag.

This doesn't mean you don't start the tasks that need starting or that you leave tasks unfinished for the sake of saving them for later. What's important is that you focus on the chief priority on the schedule of your project.

I have found that it is better to have a smaller crew working on my priority projects than to put a large crew to work completing tasks that the smaller crew should handle later on when the appropriate time comes. Effectively managing what needs to be done with a small crew means banking hours; you'll be able to draw from these hours at a later point in the project if you need to.

We talked earlier about the fact that it's easier to build up your manpower for short periods of time than to recover valuable labor hours once they've been spent, and about how there is a very fine line between having too much manpower and not enough. Your job is to figure out where that line is and stay right on it. You can do this by evaluating your manpower needs frequently and objectively.

Around the middle or latter part of a project, the tendency is to keep your eye on the finish line that is fast approaching. You may feel the urge to increase your manpower at times like this, but the reality is that it might not be necessary. Could it make your life easier in the short run? Could it ease some of the stress? Sure. But stop and ask yourself if the situation really warrants more manpower or you're taking the easy way out. Always make your decision about manpower based on what is best for the project *in the long run*.

THE BEST-LAID PLANS

Ah, the best-laid plans... We all know that plans can change, whether it's going to the movies or predicting the outcome of your project. The best we can say about change is that it is inevitably...inevitable. It's impossible to foresee everything that can or will happen on a project. What *is* within your power is always having that thorough and deliberate plan. Avoiding issues that are preventable will always put you in a better position to tackle the issues that you can't see coming.

FINAL THOUGHTS

Have the foremen you worked for in the past taken planning seriously? If not, perhaps the fact that they haven't is a product of their own experiences working with other foremen who were also poor examples. Perhaps they never had the luxury of working around a competent foreman who could teach them the importance of solid planning. Perhaps lack of a good teacher has set them up to believe they can run a good job by taking everything as it comes— and perhaps some of them might even experience a mild degree of success.

But this is not about questioning a foreman's dedication to his job. It is about asking whether he has the desire to improve or is content to merely survive from job to job.

In the end, this is about you and your career as a foreman. That's why knowing that you can never reach your true potential—run a really great job—by protecting your comfort zone is so important. My advice? Break out. Take the path of creativity and ingenuity. Seek out methods that have been proven to work or create new ones based on your experiences.

The construction industry is a competitive world and you need any edge you can get to stay ahead of the pack. The minute you rest on your laurels you open the door for someone else to step in. If you never stop learning new ways to improve your planning skills, you will never stop improving efficiency and production on each project you undertake.

ORGANIZATION

Chapter 14

Why Organization is So Important

PLANNING VS. ORGANIZATION

What is the difference between planning and organizing? Planning is making sure you have the tools, material, information, and manpower on site when you need it. Organizing is making sure every individual on your crew who needs the tool, material, and information can find it in a reasonable amount of time. Organization is about executing the plan you've put in place as efficiently and effectively as you can.

If it's the responsibility of the foreman to make sure that he and his crew work as productively as possible, then it only makes sense that it is also his responsibility to make sure his project stays organized. There is only one way to accomplish this goal: by communicating his expectations frequently and clearly to his crew and having systems in place that promote an organized job site.

On-the-Job Training: Visitors

A couple of visitors have just arrived on your job site. Your supervisor and the customer are two of them. They enter your trailer without prior notice—not even a phone call—and say, "Hope you don't mind...we were just in the neighborhood." Suddenly you're scrambling to fix the piles of paper, straighten out the wrinkled prints now held together with tape, and right the trash that's fallen on the floor by your desk. Forget about the banana peel across the room; it's too far away to reach.

This may be an exaggeration, but if your job site looks like a disaster zone, your visitors will not think twice about making judgments about you and your abilities. Subconscious or not, these judgment will have a negative affect on how you are perceived. On the other hand, if your visitors "catch you" with your prints, your trailer, your tools, your material, and even your crew organized and neat, they will be sure to go away feeling that you take pride in your work and that you have high standards. They will leave confident that you are doing your best to turn out a quality product.

Give your visitors every reason to be pleasantly surprised by the way you do things. When forming their opinions about you as a foreman, how you maintain your project is a major contributing factor.

BEING PROFESSIONAL

In the construction trades or in any other vocations, men and women who are proud of what they do want to be considered professionals. The only way to earn that label is through the consistency of your actions. Sprucing up around the job site when you know you're going to have an important visitor is not the way to go about it. It's about having pride in your site and making sure that it runs efficiently.

Are most construction sites organized and clean? Do most people who think of job sites typically think of them as dirty and unappealing or well tended and presentable? We all know the answer to these questions. Give your customers the opportunity to see you as a cut above the rest; you'll find it's another small way to get a leg up on the competition. In a competitive marketplace where multiple companies provide the same services at or around the same cost, your level of professionalism can be the thing that tips the scale in your favor. You'll never know how many opportunities that you or your company might miss based on a potential customer's less than positive perception of how you manage projects.

Remember, staying organized lessens stress and helps you continue planning for future phases of the project. Any extra time you gain will be a benefit to your success and your sanity.

Chapter 15

Organization is Everyone's Responsibility

Teams are only as strong as their weakest link. This is as true when running a construction project as it is in team sports.

The responsibility of running an efficient project falls on everyone involved with its execution. It starts with the project manager and trickles all the way down to material handlers and laborers. All it takes is one person who doesn't work to potential for your team to see all their planning and hard work diminish or dissipate. If you are a foreman who is organized and who plans in advance, you won't be pleased if someone on your team constantly drops the ball and doesn't take his responsibilities as seriously as you do.

THE WEAK LINK

What can you do when an individual on your team is not willing or able to do his part to keep the project running smoothly? The first thing is to be willing to communicate your dissatisfaction and let him know how his lack of performance is affecting the project. If you don't communicate your feelings, you can't expect anything more from this individual, even if you fool yourself into thinking he will suddenly change his ways without intervention.

Of course this is all well and good when it's a crewmember who needs the talking to. But what if it's your supervisor who isn't living up to his responsibilities? As difficult as it may be, this issue will only continue to bother you more and more over time if you do nothing about it. That means it's up to you to talk to him.

Be willing to lay out your concerns in a professional, nonconfrontational way.

Look at it like this. When you sign on as a foreman, you and your project manager have agreed to make a commitment to each other. Running a project is a joint effort on the part of many individuals. Just because someone holds a higher position than yours doesn't mean he gets to choose when and if he will be responsible. If he is not carrying his weight due to too heavy a workload, then he needs to take it up with his supervisor. No, I'm not recommending that you jump up and down and throw a fit. But you can sit down with him and lay out your concerns in a *professional, nonconfrontational* way.

Of course we have all had the experience of wanting to say something to a superior, but holding back because we're worried about making him mad. We worry it will somehow affect our employment or future opportunities to run work. Naturally, these are valid concerns; in my personal opinion, however, it is worth the risk.

Here's why. More than likely your project manager spends most of his time off site. That means that when commitments made by that same project manager aren't being met, you will be the one the customer or site superintendant comes to see. Since you are your company's representative on site every day, you are in the position of taking care of the problems that arise and fulfilling all commitments made on your company's behalf.

On-the-Job Training: The Surprise

You have done a thorough job of planning and your project and crew is organized and running efficiently. Suddenly, out of nowhere, the superintendant for the general contractor approaches you and asks why something that your project manager promised would be finished by now isn't even being worked on. He goes on to tell you that you are holding up other trades and that until you finish your work, they won't be able to get theirs done. He is unhappy and tells you he expects you to fix it. NOW.

In cases like this when you're caught unaware and feel as if there's been a surprise attack, it's normal to react with irritation, to feel aggravated and aggrieved. After all, the superintendent is demanding you take care of something that wasn't even on your radar. Perhaps it wasn't on your list of tasks to complete because your project manager is disorganized. Perhaps he doesn't communicate well...or perhaps he just plain forgot to tell you. Whatever the reason that the task didn't get the attention your supervisor thinks it deserved, however, you are now squarely in the line of fire and have to operate in a reactionary mode to appease the general contractor.

We know that working in a reactionary mode leads to inefficiency and loss of productivity. And we know that inefficiency and loss of productivity equals loss of profitability. So what can you do?

At this point, the first thing you must do is take care of the customer and general contractor. Make absolutely sure that all of their needs are being met. If this were an isolated case, I would probably never say a word to my project manager. On the other hand, if it became a trend, I'd probably choose to speak with him and let him know how I feel. It's either that or accept the way he does things and prepare to be frustrated by frequent unforeseen events.

Unfortunately, issues like these don't usually work themselves out on their own. That's why they need to be handled in a professional and constructive manner. I suggest calling your project manager and asking to have a sit-down meeting in a location where you can talk one on one, preferably away from the job site.

Remember to come prepared to any meeting you arrange. You are the one who has requested the meeting, and this is your chance to put it all out on the table. Use the opportunity wisely. If you have to write your thoughts down beforehand then do it. Pointing your finger and being insulting will only serve to instantly put your project manager on the defensive. Instead, explain what your challenges are and how the project is suffering for those challenges.

Come prepared. Come with solutions.

Bring possible solutions to the table as well. Always be willing to take his suggestions, but make sure by the end of the meeting it is very clear what you need in terms of his support. Hopefully the outcome will be that your project manager understands your concerns and is willing to work with you to move forward in the right direction.

Based on my own experience, I believe that if you deal with the situation as outlined above, most times you will have a positive outcome. With that said, there will always be those people who think that being in a position of authority means it is their job to tell you what to do and not the other way around. Of course this kind of thinking is ego-driven and counterproductive to a good working relationship with subordinates.

Still, not everyone sees it this way. If you come across a project manager like this sometime in your career I suggest you simply finish whatever commitment you have with them and then politely decline to work for them in the future. You have to believe in yourself and be confident that the skills you bring to the table are worthy of respect. Furthermore, when you possess the skills of a competent and highly qualified foreman you will have no problem finding a contractor who will need you as much as you need them.

CONSTRUCTION INDUSTRY PLAYERS

Running a project efficiently and productively takes the efforts of many different people in many different positions. Contractors will have their own ideas about who should take care of which responsibilities and you will need to adapt as necessary. Below I've provided some general information about the typical roles of each person on a construction team.

MANAGEMENT

Organization always starts at the top, with management. Unorganized management teams are much more likely to have unorganized foremen. Management is expected to keep their responsibilities and commitments organized while setting a good example for those in their employ. It would be out of line and hypocritical for management to tell their subordinates what to do and expect them to do it if they are not themselves setting the appropriate example. "Do as I say, not as I do" may work with children, but it doesn't work with adults who are looking to their leader for guidance.

It is inevitable that at some point in your career you will work for someone in management who is not well organized. This creates problems and makes your job much more difficult. But don't let this situation compromise your commitment to the project. There are ways of dealing with these issues and the frustrations they create. In the short term it's in your best interest to maintain your dedication to make the project a success until a resolution can be reached—or you move onto another company's employ.

For starters, project managers are responsible for having a set of up-to-date blueprints for all projects in their domain. Next, all pertinent project documentation, such as project specifications, need to accurately match those of the foreman and the customer. All items need to be easily accessible for quick reference should a foreman or the customer call for verification, something that is not an uncommon occurrence.

If the project manager needs to dig through piles of paper to find what should be close at hand, it only slows things down and gives the impression to the foreman (or worse, to the customer) that the manager is not wholly invested in the project. Not only will this be frustrating for you if you are the foreman, but if the customer is the one on the phone, he may come away with the feeling he is not important to your company. This can have a lasting negative effect and will most certainly influence the customer's decision whether to do business with your company in the future.

Customers who feel neglected simply go away.

Keep in mind that customers who feel unimportant or neglected generally do not make an announcement that your company has lost credibility and their trust. They simply go away.

Speaking from a foreman's point of view, before I agree to run a project I need to know that I will have a project manager who is supportive and involved and who understands the complexities of my project. Although project managers are expected to multi-task by managing several different projects at once, it is imperative they have a solid working knowledge of each and every project.

SUPERINTENDANT/GENERAL FOREMAN

As a superintendent or general foreman it is your responsibility to make sure that all of the foremen and their crews work together to maintain an organized job site. Just like management, it is the general foreman's responsibility to hold his foremen accountable for the way they run their individual crews. A good general foreman will be in constant communication with all the leaders on his team and will make clear what challenges they face and how they will meet those challenges.

This action has to start at the very beginning of every project and continue to the end. A project that starts out unorganized will only become harder to manage as the crews get larger and the demand for material and tools increase.

Because general foremen attend many more coordination and planning meetings than their field foremen, they need to thoroughly communicate the information they receive to their foremen. For this reason, it is absolutely crucial they meet with their foremen regularly to verify that everyone is aware of the upcoming phases of the project.

Frequent meetings are also a good way to make sure that future phases of the project are not being ignored. On big jobs, when all the foremen are going in different directions, things can easily fall through the cracks. If something has been overlooked or there is a phase of the project that hasn't been delegated to a foreman, it will eventually become apparent in one of these meetings.

Meetings also provide an opportunity to hash out any problems foremen may be having with each other in the field. This is the perfect opportunity for the general foreman to address issues and find solutions before they hinder job progress. General foremen miss valuable opportunities to keep their project running in the right direction if they don't continually pull their team together and communicate their overall plans and expectations.

FOREMAN

The foreman's top priorities are planning and organization for himself and his crew. His crew's ability to be efficient and productive relies heavily on their being able to find what they need to do their job as quickly as possible.

A foreman's job is to make it clear to the crew what their role is in keeping an organized job site. All it takes to derail a well-conceived plan are one or two crewmembers who refuse to keep things orderly and organized. Before long the whole crew gives up—and no one likes to follow behind his coworkers and pick up after them. Combat this tendency by frequently discussing the importance of organization with your crew. It may take some repetition, but you have to start somewhere.

You might decide to designate an apprentice or laborer to be responsible for spending a little extra time every day to make sure everything is stored in a neat and orderly fashion. You will be money ahead when your crewmembers can always find what they need quickly and easily. Remember, time lost is money lost.

Don't be surprised when there are times when you feel like throwing in the towel and give up on your efforts to keep an organized site because the task is so daunting, especially during the peak of your material and manpower needs. At these times, I would encourage you to consider what is at stake.

For example, recently I was working for another foreman as a journeyman and was consistently having trouble finding what I needed without taking lots of time to find it. The material was scattered around the site, the gang boxes in which our tools were stored were a disaster, and the morale of the crew was in bad shape.

It was late in the project and staying organized had never been a topic of discussion throughout the length of the job. I therefore took the risk of telling the foreman that I was really having trouble completing tasks because I couldn't always find what I needed. He acknowledged there was "definitely a problem," but responded by saying that he had given up on trying. In my head I was saying, "*What?! You've given up?!*"

First of all, a foreman who admits defeat to one of his crewmembers does not instill confidence. Second, by saying he had given up, the foreman is implying that he had at some point made some kind of effort to keep the project organized. In this case, I guess it's possible that the foreman periodically opened up the gang boxes and pushed some things around to make them seem a bit more organized,...or perhaps went to the shelves of miscellaneous material himself...or perhaps even asked someone to put things away or clean things up from time to time. But the result was no different from telling a child to clean his room and then finding everything has been shoved under the bed. The room might appear to be clean at first glance, but sooner or later the under-the-bed approach will reveal its obvious flaws.

Had this foreman addressed his crew from the outset of the project and communicated his expectations he would have given the project a fighting chance. As it was, the project ended up in the red, and it is my belief that his being so unorganized largely contributed to that result.

As with the general foreman and the project manager, leading by example is the only way to ensure your crew will believe in your methods. Be sure, be straightforward, and be consistent.

CREW (JOURNEYMEN AND APPRENTICES)

Having a good crew that works as a team can make or break a job. It starts with a crew that is informed as to what is expected of them. When foremen are frustrated with their crew over things like organization, however, they often fail to realize that they are partially to blame.

In my opinion, it should be common sense that organization is an important tool, but my many years of experience in the industry have proven over and over that it is not. And knowing this is only half the battle. There are just too many people who don't care, don't think it is part of their job, are lazy, or don't think it is worth the trouble. It is up to you to convince them otherwise.

When you are the boss, it is your responsibility to explain why you are asking these individuals to cooperate. Communicating what your organizational expectations are sets a standard to which your crew can be held accountable.

You can't expect people to read your mind. Not only that, many members of your crew may not ever have worked for foremen who required them to participate in maintaining the organization of a job site. This means a constant diligence on your part to let them know what you need from them. The reality is that there are a lot of people who will do no more and no less than what is asked of them. It's just how some people operate. Rather than being irritated by this attitude, make sure to inform them of what they can do to help you out. If they can't or won't participate in what you ask, then you may have to make the decision to remove them from your project. You can't let one person affect the way your entire project is run.

MATERIAL HANDLERS AND LABORERS

Material handlers and laborers are just as important as anyone else. Without them you have a lot less likelihood that your project will stay organized and run smoothly because they are often the ones who supply the project with tools and material and make sure everything gets where it needs to be. They are the ones you will ask (and expect) to take extra care in the organization of these tools and material. These crewmembers are as valuable to you and the success of your project as everyone else.

Material handlers can make a big impact on a project based on their attitude and how they approach their job. Once again it falls on the foreman to explain their role. If you or the rest of your crew treat them as if they are the lowest on the totem pole and not worthy of respect, then you should expect nothing more than a mediocre performance from them. We all want to be appreciated for what we bring to the game, no matter how large or small our contribution.

Encourage them by showing your appreciation and by giving them advice on how to further their career whenever possible. Unless you were born with a silver spoon in your mouth, you've started out like the rest of us—at the bottom in the construction industry. Everyone appreciates helpful advice to get where they want to be.

On-the-job Training: Handling It Right

You are the foreman on a project. You discover you need a specific tool from your shop so you send your material handler over to pick it up. You know that there are plenty of individuals who think nothing of walking over, grabbing the tool off the shelf, and heading back to the job site without first checking to make sure the tool is in good working order. However, you feel very comfortable knowing that this won't happen on your site because you have taught your material handlers well.

You have not only impressed on them the importance of checking every step they take and their importance to the success of your project, but you have also shown them appreciation for the work they do. You know that they are therefore more inclined to pay close attention to detail and do the extra things that will make your job easier and less stressful.

This is a good example of how a material handler who feels like an integral part of your team can save you time, money, and considerable aggravation.

VENDORS

A vendor who provides great customer service and understands the challenges you frequently face is an invaluable resource. The problem is that many vendors promise you the world to get your business, but then fall way short of the mark in their performance. This can create big problems for you. You rely heavily on your vendors to get supplies to you when and where you need them and at a price that keeps you competitive. If you sacrifice service to save a dollar, you may find yourself holding the bag in the end.

Before getting deep into a project you and your management team should sit down with all the representatives of the vendors who will be supplying your project. Establish the contacts for your company and for theirs. Set parameters for what you expect from them and what they should expect from you. Try to provide them with quantities of any long-lead or special-order items you will need along with when you will need them on site. Inform them of any special instructions for deliveries, including specific windows of time for deliveries, driver requirements for coming on site, and any other unique challenges your project may have. These meetings are very important because they create a record of what each person has agreed their responsibilities will be *before* the heavy pressures of the project set in.

FINAL THOUGHTS

Running an organized project takes the whole team and the whole team's effort. Because you have the most at stake, it's important for you to lead this effort. Staying on top of your game by making sure everyone on the project fulfills his responsibilities will ensure you can fulfill your own responsibilities and keep your project running steadily and fluently.

Chapter 16

Organizational Challenges

If all it takes to stay organized is a foreman who tells his crew to put things back where they get them and to throw their trash away once in a while, every project would be a piece of cake. But it takes much more than that.

A well-run project takes a concerted effort by the foreman to put systems in place that enable the crew to start out organized and stay organized. Two things are necessary:

1. That you have organization permanently in the forefront of your mind as you begin your project and that you know it is as important as anything else you do.

2. That you consistently use good communication skills to empower the crew to do whatever is necessary to maintain an organized site with you and for you.

There are plenty of foremen who never even address this issue. Some perceive it as someone else's job; others see it as unimportant. But bad habits produce substandard results. Just like planning, organization is a key element in your long-term level of success.

Organization requires your early, focused, and consistent attention.

It's too easy to be consumed by other responsibilities that require your immediate attention. Don't make the mistake of sloughing off organizational issues to the side because you believe you'll find time later to focus on them after the project ramps up. This will never happen.

On-the-Job Training: Disorganized?

You are the foreman on a site that has become disorganized. Tools and materials often have to be tracked down to be used by your crewmembers. You can often be heard to say, "I know I ordered that tool; it has to be here somewhere." Your general *modus operandi* is to expect your employees to track down the missing tool or material (or send them to track it down).

Each time someone needs a tool, the same thing happens: you need to send a crewmember on another trip around the job site to locate it. Finding the tool can take a few minutes or an hour; you just never know.

> However, because everyone on the crew is so busy, because it would be a lot of work, and because you don't feel particularly motivated, you don't take the initiative to reorganize the site to keep the same scenario from occurring again. You let it go again.
>
> The next time it happens, you wish you'd done what you needed to do to change the outcome.

Does this sound like you? I know it probably seems like beating a dead horse on the subject of wasted labor and how it affects the bottom line, but in order to be a great foreman, you have to understand that every single decision you make has the potential to increase or decrease production.

Just think about the employee who's wandering your job site looking for a tool. What do think happens after you send him off in search of what he needs? If you're lucky, he'll find it quickly and get right back to work. But we all know that's not the norm. Generally, he won't find it quickly and/or won't get right back work. He won't volunteer to tell you how long it took and you'll probably never find out how much time was spent in the process. What you have inadvertently done is provided your employee with a free pass to roam the project in search of something he may or may not find.

Furthermore, as your employee continues to wander from floor to floor looking for this missing tool and asking other workers if they've seen it, he may get caught up in conversations about what he's doing the upcoming weekend or about the football game the night before. The group may get into a heated discussion about the fact that they can never find what they need to get their job done. Time goes by.

At this point, if you come along and see a couple of employees who appear to be doing nothing more than visiting, what do you say? You might ask the employee you'd sent to look for the tool, "What are you doing over here? I thought you were working on another floor." To which they might well respond, "Don't you remember, you sent me to look for it. I haven't found it yet." It's pretty tough to argue with that.

WASTE MAKES...WASTE

Along with the direct wasted labor of this one employee, you also have to figure in how the lack of organization will affect crew morale, which in turn will likely decrease production. Every disgruntled employee has the ability to drag other employees down. We will discuss people skills further in Part 4.

The funny thing about disorganization is that it gathers momentum like a snowball. Once it starts rolling down the hill it becomes nearly impossible to rein in and get under control. When planning a new project, the following tips can assist you in tackling organizational challenges.

LOCATE STAGING AREAS

The day you start looking through the blueprints is the day you should start to identify spaces inside the floor print of the project for potential staging areas for your tools and materials. Look for areas that are large and open. If possible, these locations should be close to areas where you will have a lot of work and centrally located in order to cut down on your crew's travel time as they gather up what they need for their individual tasks.

Here are a few things to consider as you identify your staging areas:

» Do the locations have easy access for deliveries when they arrive?

» Are there any height or width restrictions that will create problems along the path to your staging area from the area where the delivery of supplies is made?

» Is this location in an area that will cause you to move multiple times in order for the other trades to have access to complete their tasks throughout the length of the project?

Once you've settled on a potential area, communicate your thoughts with the other trades and the general contractor. This establishes your intent and gives the other foremen a chance to let you know if there is any plausible reason why the area you've chosen might not be a good idea. Remember, *you* want to be driving this conversation. Don't be the foreman who sits on the sidelines waiting to get stuck with locations no one else wants. This will only leave you and your crew at a disadvantage.

Now that your staging area has been set, get your gang boxes and material racks in place as soon as possible. A space left wide open is an invitation for another trade to move in. Having a crew move to another location after they have laid claim to an area only creates the potential for friction and tension between trades.

After you have obtained and organized everything your crew could possibly need and have set yourself up in a convenient location, your next challenge begins.

STAYING FIRM

It's now time to convince your crew of the importance of taking the same care and concern to keep things organized that was established while setting the project up. If you can win your crew over to your way of thinking your project will stand a much better chance of success. I know it's easier said than done, but that doesn't mean there is any excuse to surrender. Stay firm on your position that you will not tolerate a messy and unorganized site! It may take many conversations and regular reminders, but do not slack off on your commitment.

Crewmembers bring with them as many good and bad habits and attitudes as there are individuals. They have picked up all sorts of work-related routines learned from all their previous combined projects. It's not that they won't be willing to do what is being asked of them necessarily, but that they may not be accustomed to your way of doing it. Encourage them to believe in what you are trying to accomplish through good communication and positive reinforcement.

FINAL THOUGHTS

As you find and implement solutions to your organizational problems, you will watch production increase and crew morale rise, and you will find yourself with more time to focus on the day-to-day tasks and issues that you encounter.

Chapter 17

Organization and Safety

Along with good planning, maintaining an organized job site creates a much safer site and an overall better work environment.

Organizing and storing all safety equipment and devices in a readily accessible location is one of the first steps toward running a safe job. Unfortunately, a typical scenario looks more like this: The foreman orders safety equipment. It gets used once. It ends up misplaced or stuffed in a gang box where it can be lost or damaged.

To combat this lackadaisical attitude you need your crew to understand your expectations. Once again it's all about communicating very clearly what you need from them—and not just once, but as many times as it takes. When your crew mishandles tools or material it can make your life more difficult, but when they're not working safely due to organizational issues things become a matter of life and death.

It should be obvious, therefore, that good organization improves safety. When your crew knows where to find the safety equipment, and they know that when they find it, it will be in good working order, they are more likely to use it. It's that simple. On the other hand, if your crew believes that they're going to have to search high and low through the entire job site to find a piece of safety gear when they're starting their task, they are more likely to take a chance and skip using the appropriate safety measures altogether.

DON'T WAIT

If you wait for someone on your crew to bring up all the safety concerns that need to be addressed, you may have to wait a long time. As mentioned earlier, ignoring safety concerns means accidents. Those who know there's a problem but choose not to express it are generally concerned about the negative attention they feel they'll get from their foreman if they do. It's up to you to assure them that this will not be the case and that your first concern is their safety and wellbeing.

Assuring them your first concern is their safety means telling them that you are counting on them to spot safety concerns and that you encourage them to bring any issues to your attention. Doing this opens up a dialogue in which the crew feels it can participate. Often such dialogues inspire the crew to find solutions to the problems, which also contributes to a feeling of empowerment and morale on the job.

THE REPRIMAND

Part of creating a safe work environment is holding your employees accountable when they choose to take unnecessary risks. Nobody enjoys reprimanding someone who is trying to get the job done. Unfortunately, it has to be done. You can't set the precedence that you are willing to look the other way for the sake of production. If you ignore the fact that someone is working unsafely even once and your crew sees you do it, you immediately slip down a few notches on the pole of credibility.

I'm not suggesting that you fire someone on the spot or embarrass him in front of the other crewmembers. I am suggesting you take him aside and talk to him. Make it clear that although production is important, it isn't important enough for him to be get hurt or killed. Explain how an accident will affect his family both financially and emotionally if the worst were to happen. Reiterate your commitment to safety to him and let him know that safety is a team effort and you are counting on his help.

INVINCIBILITY

There will always be individuals who feel they are invincible. These tend to be the same individuals who choose not to wear safety gear because they don't see the need for it. You need to deal with these people swiftly and effectively. Idle threats don't get it done.

When unsafe workers are doing the same tasks as those who are taking the time to do it safely, they are setting an example for your crew that you can't afford. Because those who aren't taking the time to do their jobs safely are often slightly more productive than the rest of the crew, the other crewmembers may start cutting corners to compete. After all, they don't want to appear inefficient next to their coworker. This speaks to the fact that no matter what anyone says, construction workers are quite aware that production is king and that the best and most productive workers stay employed on a consistent basis.

Armed with this knowledge, you should always be looking for the signs an employee is working unsafely to gain an edge. As tempting as it is to let safety slide a little bit in order to move the job along, you are the only one who can draw a hard line in the sand.

FINAL THOUGHTS

The reason many job sites are dirty, messy, disorganized, and/ or unsafe is because this has been the norm in the construction business since the beginning of time. Most construction workers believe it's just the way things are done because they've seen it done that way from the very beginning of their career. When you hear, "How can we keep it clean when we are constantly surrounded by so much dust and debris?" your answer should be, "It's not about keeping the site spotless as far as the dust and dirt are concerned. It's about keeping the tools, material, and safety equipment in order so we can continue to work in areas that aren't cluttered by piles of material and debris."

There is no excuse for having your site in total disarray. Can you imagine a manufacturing facility allowing miscellaneous tools and material to be spread across the site without any sort of semblance of order? Of course not. Everything has a place where it can fulfill its function in the process. People on production lines are not sent on aimless searches through their factories to find the things they need to do their job. Why should it be any different with construction?

The bottom line is that organization is a choice. Every project presents yet another opportunity for the foreman to create organizational standards that will ultimately improve every project's chance for maximum production and success.

IV

PEOPLE SKILLS

Chapter 18

People Skills at Work

So far this book has focused on understanding the contracting business, the importance of good planning, and on making organization a priority, and I have reiterated that none of these aspects is more important than any other. But what you will learn in the following chapters regarding people skills may be the most critical element of all to become a successful foreman.

In construction, those who work for you are your biggest asset. You will continually interact with people of many different backgrounds, skill levels, mind sets, and personalities. Treat them right, and they will work hard for you. Treat them poorly, and I promise you it will be an ongoing struggle to achieve your career goals.

Throughout my career I have been witness to foremen who possess every technical skill necessary to build just about anything, but who have remained stagnant in their careers. Meanwhile, foremen who are far less talented at the technical aspect of their job have passed the others by when promotions became available.

What did the latter understand that the former did not? I would venture to say that savvy foremen know that being the smartest and most technically sound craftsman in your trade does not automatically make you a good foreman, and that having strong technical skills coupled with the ability to inspire your crew to work hard is the key.

Good foremen want their crews to achieve success right along side of them.

Good foremen know that treating their crew disrespectfully or ruling them with an iron fist and still expecting them to perform at the peak performance never works. Treating people poorly only leads to discontent, and a disgruntled workforce will never want to see you, let alone help you, realize your goals. In fact, they may even go out of their way to make sure that you don't.

You don't have to be a psychologist or a pushover to be a great foreman, but it is necessary to acknowledge that not everyone learns the same way, works the same way, or sees their job the same way that you do. Finding a way to work well with a variety of different personalities while encouraging individuals to reach their potential builds a loyal following of dedicated employees who respect and admire you. This earned respect and admiration equates to better efficiency, better productivity, and a strong overall appreciation for you as a leader.

Part Four is dedicated to sharing the best ways to positively motivate your employees to do an exceptional job for you. I have provided examples of how to make this happen, as well as examples of what can happen when your crew does not feel connected to either you or your methods. At the conclusion of this section you will possess the tools to communicate effectively, motivate those around you, and, most importantly, to understand what is at the heart of being a great foreman.

Chapter 19

Perception

We all use perception in everyday life to make judgments about the people we meet. We take what we have been told and then add what we see, hear, and experience of an individual to generate an image in our minds of what we should expect from him. Sometimes the conclusions we reach are a fair assessment, while other times our predetermined feelings turn out to be less than accurate—in other words, more fiction than fact. The problem comes when we behave in a way that matches our preconceived judgment, which may be way off the mark.

This is an important concept because at the same time we are using our perception and judgment to rate our crew and their abilities, they are also using their perception and judgment to make conclusions about us and our abilities. It's true what they say about the importance of making a good first impression, but it's the way we are perceived and perceive others *over time* that matters most.

Perception is powerful. It can override a person's logical thinking and be driven strictly by emotion. For example, if you instantly take offense at the way a new crewmember dresses or wears his hair when he first shows up on your site, it's a short step to unconsciously making other judgments about that individual, ones which likely have no merit in terms of his work ethic or whether he will do a good job for you. The fact that you are jumping to conclusions may never enter your mind, but if your observations coupled with someone else's previous comments about this individual affect your attitude, you might form a lesser opinion of him before you have even been introduced.

IT'S A TWO-WAY STREET

Assumptions and perceptions are a two-way street. In my career, I have always been well aware of the reputation of the foremen with whom I know I'll be working. All it takes is a couple of phone calls to coworkers and in no time at all I have begun to form my opinion.

What does this tell you? That when you are the foreman, your new employees will likely be doing the same thing, and showing up with an image of you that may not be very flattering. For instance, they may have come from another project where one of their coworkers told them you were an untrustworthy and unorganized foreman. True or not, if that's the image they have you will instantly be put in the position of having to prove yourself to be trustworthy and organized.

Naturally, there is no way to know for sure what preconceived ideas will be out there about you. That's why it's important to understand that every decision you make, starting with how you treat your employees, will be judged based on the perceptions—founded or not—by those around you.

Just knowing and acknowledging the role perception plays is only half the battle, however. The other half is continually proving yourself to every new employee with whom you come in contact. By displaying good planning, organization, and people skills you will ultimately prove to anyone who questions your abilities that you are, in fact, a capable leader worthy of respect.

On-the-Job Training: Relationships at Work

Are you a foreman who continually finds himself in the position where the perceptions of others are affecting your work-related relationships? Do you hear yourself taking the attitude, "What do I care what people think? I'm the boss. I don't care if people like or respect me. If they don't like me or the way I do things then they can hit the bricks."

It's convenient to fall into this mind set if you have questionable leadership skills coupled with difficulties maintaining a good rapport with your crew.

The first thing that comes to my mind when I hear a foreman saying something like this is that I don't believe him. I simply do not believe that people don't care if they are respected on the job. It's human nature to want to be liked and respected, and it's not something you can turn off just because you're at work. Those who can turn it off are generally not people we want to be around anyway. I think this kind of attitude stems more from insecurity than anything else, and from the inability to handle tough situations.

FINAL THOUGHTS

In summary, this "my way or the highway" approach doesn't work. It has never has worked and it never will work. Operating from this perspective eventually equates to poor morale, poor communication, poor efficiency, poor production, and ultimately to poor profitability for your company. The irony is that your responsibility as a foreman is to make sure that all these aspects of the job are maintained at the highest level possible.

Basically, it comes down to this: You either learn how to work well with people and prove to them through your actions that you are a good leader, or you face a long uphill battle that leaves you struggling to be successful every step of the way.

Chapter 20

Earning Respect

I considered naming this chapter with one word: "Respect." But after some reflection on its meaning relative to my career in the industry, I felt the title needed more clarification because, in my opinion, the word has been so twisted and distorted that its true meaning has become blurred.

In the construction industry the word "respect" gets thrown around so often that we have become numb to its meaning. "Respect your coworkers." "Respect the other trades." "Respect your journeyman." "Respect your foreman." "Respect management." It's as if from the minute you enter the construction industry you are supposed to instantly respect and trust anyone who got there before you. To this philosophy, I ask, *Whatever happened to the concept of actually earning the respect of others?*

Would you respect someone outside the workplace just because you were told you should? Of course not. You form your own opinions based on the individual's reputation and actions. So, why should work be any different?

I do believe that a certain level of deference should come automatically to any individual who has been in the business longer than I have or who holds a position of authority. What I don't buy into is automatically offering a high level of respect to individuals who assume that their position gives them that right; that their egos deserve to be stroked by their subordinates—whether they have earned it or not.

Frankly, anyone who enters this industry with the illusion that respect comes automatically with rank and title changes is in for a big surprise. The only real path to respect is through exhibiting professional qualities and proving yourself to those on your team.

This is a good time to ask yourself the following questions:

> » What kinds of experiences have you had so far in the industry that are related to respect—either given or received?

> » Have you worked for individuals who would other-wise be good foremen if their people skills were a little more polished?

> » Has your own production or loyalty decreased when you worked for someone you didn't respect?

> » How have you noticed that your attitude changes when you work for someone whom you hold in high regard?

At some point in your career you may reach the point of receiving respect solely on your reputation, but it is a long and arduous path to reaching this status. Of the foremen I have worked with over the last 20 years I would put only about 5% into this category. This is not to say the other 95% were terrible at every aspect of their job, but the level of respect they carried from project to project was not where it could have been. What is most unfortunate for them is that the lack of respect they receive continually negatively impacts the results of every project they run.

If you are interested in being the best foreman you can be, one of your primary objectives has to be having the respect of your peers and employees. When people respect you, not only will they work hard for you, but they will also advocate for you. When the people who know and respect you are willing to endorse you as a great foreman to fellow coworkers or your management team, you will consistently feel the positive influence their respect has on your career.

On-the-Job Training: The Customer

You have just finished a couple of difficult projects in a hospital. On these jobs there were many challenges with the continuing operation of the hospital as you and your crew completed your work. You worked hard to listen to all of your customer's concerns and to make sure you adhered to every policy and request they made, all with minimal disruption to their facility and its function.

At the conclusion of these projects, the customer sent a letter to your company, thanking it for the foreman's attention to detail and concern for the special needs they had. In their final statement, they requested that you be the foreman on any future projects.

Does this sound too good to be true? I can guarantee you, it does happen—to those who have the respect and reputation for following through and getting the job done right.

At the beginning of every project there is always someone promising the customer the world. It might be the project manager or maybe the foreman himself. At that point, everyone is ready to hit the ground running with what appears to be the best of intentions. What frequently follows, however, is a cycle of mistakes and apologies that results in a disappointed and frustrated customer. This not only leads to lost respect for the foreman, but for the contractor as well. Unhappy customers become used to hearing lies and getting the run-around from contractors and foremen.

If you give your customers what they need and want, but very seldom find... If you strive to become the one individual they can count on... You and your company are likely to have a steady income for years to come.

BATTLING THE EGO

For anyone who suffers from an overinflated ego, here is a word of advice. If the people who work for you think you are a tyrant with an ego the size of Texas, they're sure to talk about you when you're not around. People love to take jabs at those in authority if there has been the slightest provocation. It's human nature to jabber on and complain about others to those with a sympathetic ear. Don't give these people a motive! If your ego is compromising your management skills, reconsider what's at stake before you blame others for your inadequacies.

Unfortunately, most people are more prone to talk about their superiors to complain than to hail their virtues. Though it's true that if people like and respect you they will speak highly of you, it's more likely that your name will be heard more often when they're blowing off steam, especially if you have belittled them in some way.

And here's some more bad news. If even one person on your crew doesn't like you then it is probably safe to say that the rest of the crew feels the same way. This produces a large number of willing participants having conversations where the sole purpose is to vent about how they wish they could tell you off. Sounds to me like a recipe for disaster.

A bad reputation spreads like wild fire.

Getting a wild fire of gossip under control can take a very long time and conscious effort on your part. That's why, especially if you are a new foreman starting out, I suggest you establish a good working relationship with your employees that is built on mutual respect. If you are a seasoned foreman who struggles in this area, know that it is never too late to turn things around. You have to start somewhere. Once you show your employees you are willing to change and that you are committed to the change as evidenced by your doing things in a different way, you will be pleasantly surprised by the positive reaction of the people around you.

EARNING RESPECT

If you make a genuine attempt to implement the ideas below, you will have no problem earning the trust and respect you need to become a great leader. If these suggestions seem like common sense or appear elementary I apologize, but stating the obvious can be the best way to communicate the point.

RESPECTING OTHERS

Respecting others is first and foremost. If you think back on your childhood I'm sure you can remember being told to apply the Golden Rule—to treat others as you would like to be treated yourself. Sounds easy. But somewhere between being a child and becoming an adult many of us have a tendency to lose sight of this very basic and easy-to-follow concept.

As it relates to the construction industry, I have a few ideas about why this is the case. First, there are very few, if any, individuals who find their way into a foreman or project manager position without first putting in their time out in the trenches doing the grunt work. In all trades there is commonly an apprenticeship of some sort that may take as little as one year or as many as five years to complete. While this on-the-job education is what makes you a well-trained and viable candidate for a foreman position, your experiences as an apprentice or journeyman can negatively impact how you see authority and the so-called food chain.

If your time coming up through the ranks of apprentice to journeyman to foreman has been spent around foremen and management who talk down to their workers and rule with fear, intimidation, and threats, then you are more than likely to repeat those behaviors. I have known many throughout my career who have fallen into this trap. "This is how I was treated when I was first in the business. Now it's my turn to dish it out." This antiquated way of thinking only perpetuates a counter-productive method of leading a crew, one that diminishes your credibility as a professional.

Old-timers in the industry love to tell stories about how poorly they were treated when they first entered the trade. Stories of getting screamed at, humiliated, and threatened with their job abound. Some of them still believe this kind of treatment makes you strong and that you'll end up soft if you are treated any differently as you learn your craft. To those individuals I say, "This isn't the 1920s anymore, and we aren't in the Great Depression." And even if that time came around again (and we all hope it never will) workers deserve the same respect we'd like ourselves.

It is in the best interest of any foreman or contractor and essential to the positive outcome of the project that a working environment be created where people enjoy coming to work and feel they are an important part of a successful team effort. Long-term success for you and your company hinges on building a loyal group of well-trained individuals who provide you with the kind of stability and consistency that makes your job as a foreman less demanding and more satisfying.

DISRESPECT

Disrespect is also exhibited as a matter of course when someone new comes into a trade and has limited knowledge and skills. Once you have been in your trade a long time it is easy to forget where you came from, and that at one point you were just as inexperienced as the new guy is now. But acting as if you were born with the skills of your trade for the mere sake of embarrassing or belittling someone shows more ignorance than anything else.

Showing compassion and patience, on the other hand, reveals the fact that you are above that kind of slander. Don't forget, it's hard enough to start a new job without a journeyman or foreman barking about an obvious lack of knowledge.

Since every person you meet in the construction business is someone you are likely to work with again some time down the road, this bit of advice is well worth the space on this page. I know when I became a foreman I had more than a few people come to work for me who had once been my journeymen when I'd been an apprentice.

Respect is a social contract between two people. When one person is unwilling to participate it destroys any opportunity for the relationship to succeed. Whether it is a working relationship or a personal one, mutual respect sets the foundation.

FEAR IS NOT RESPECT

Another common mistake is believing that someone who is intimidated by you or fears you actually respects you. I can assure you that someone who feels this way would prefer to be working for someone else and will have no desire to see you become successful.

Naturally, having the authority to fire people or make their jobs more difficult means you hold a measure of power over them. But don't use this power to pump up your ego or to motivate through browbeating. Use your authority only when it relates to your function as a foreman to make decisions about the project you are running or when it is necessary to deal with an employee who does something requiring disciplinary action.

PERSONAL DIFFERENCES

Finally, set personal differences aside. No one agrees with everyone at work and no one has the same interests as everyone at work.

Construction workers are a diverse group of individuals who come from many walks of life. This means you will often be in the position of working with people who don't share the same hobbies, religious beliefs, political views, or philosophies.

Look at these differences as an opportunity to get an alternative perspective on a subject. When you can't find any common ground, take the high road. Choose not to engage in conversations that may weaken an otherwise functional working relationship.

TAKING RESPONSIBILITY

The transition from being a worker to a foreman can be bewildering. Suddenly you have become the intermediary between your crew and everyone else. How you handle this change will partially determine the level of respect you attain.

When you agree to take on the role of a foreman there is an enormous amount of responsibility that comes with it. You are no longer just another person on the crew who can just show up, put in your eight, and go home. Consider the way your mentality has to adjust as you take on this shift in responsibility.

First of all, your company expects you will you do everything within your power to ensure that a reasonable amount of profit will be made from the project. Secondly, you are the sole interpreter of the prints; as such you are responsible for knowing everything there is to know about your project from start to finish. Third, you are expected to be a leader, a coach, a decision maker, and a mediator for your crew. Last, you are challenged with running the most efficient and productive job possible, all while making sure your crew works safely.

To be an effective and successful foreman it is essential that you possess thick skin, broad shoulders, a self-motivating drive, multi-tasking capabilities, and a can-do attitude. Bring anything less to your role as a leader to any project and that project will surely produce less than optimum results.

How does taking responsibility apply to having a thick skin and all the rest? When you run work, *you* are the one who bears the burden of criticism that may come from your direct supervisors or the other trades on your project. *You* are the one who is held accountable when you or your crew makes a mistake.

No one likes to be in the line of fire when things go wrong. That's why, for some, it's easier to redirect the blame to those around them, thus saving themselves from any negative attention. But should you choose to skirt the responsibility that comes with your position you will find it nearly impossible to earn the respect you want and need.

THE 5% FOREMAN

There are very few foremen who can see enough of the big picture, have enough confidence in their abilities, and possess a keen enough awareness of their value to their company to unselfishly put themselves on the line for their crew. These foremen belong to a small group that can bank on the respect of individuals they have never met. Through the consistency of their actions, they have proven to be leaders their crews can rely on when the chips are down. Foremen meeting this standard are like our foreman in the following story and someone I refer to as a 5%-er.

On-the-job Training: The 5% Foreman

One day a foreman was running a project when someone on his crew broke an expensive tool. The foreman called his project manager to let him know what had happened and told him the tool would need to be replaced.

A few hours later the project manager called the foreman back to inform him that the company owner (who was known to be an unreasonable hot-head) was angry. He wanted the name of the person who broke the tool. The foreman simply replied, "If he wants someone's name, give him mine."

Why would a 5% foreman respond like this? Obviously he hadn't broken the tool. I believe it is because he knew it had been an accident and he consciously made the decision not to put his worker in the position of probable disciplinary action for attempting to do his job. A 5% foreman is comfortable in his assessment that he will not personally get chewed out or fired over something so minute, and that taking responsibility for his crewmember is the correct approach.

The story about this foreman is a true one. But I didn't hear the story from the foreman himself. I heard the details of the event from someone else who happened to be working nearby when it took place. People who know this story don't miss an opportunity to share it because they continue to be impressed by this foreman's selflessness. By my estimation, there are roughly only 5% of foremen who might behave in this manner; hence my description of our foreman as a 5%-er.

People want to believe in the leaders they follow. They want to work for someone who puts loyalty and integrity above the need to look good for their boss.

For every story like this one there are 20 more about foremen who make it their business to stay far removed from all problems and controversy. Stories about these foremen are told, too, and continue to be passed around from one individual to another.

PASSING THE BUCK

When you are faced with a situation where it would be easier for you to pass the buck to someone else, remember this: First, your supervisor will still hold you responsible for the mistakes of your crew and will duly note the lack of integrity displayed by your actions. From the supervisor's point of view, you were asked to be, and have agreed to be, the responsible party on the project.

Second, any crew that get the impression their foreman will throw them under the bus when the pressure turns up will begin to hide problems and choose to be other than forthcoming when mistakes are made.

How can you expect to earn respect or run a successful project when people see you this way?

No one expects you to be everywhere at once to verify that everyone is doing his job exactly as you have asked him to or that all of your plans are working to perfection. What they do expect is that you will stand behind the decisions you make and stand alongside your crew when something goes wrong.

BEING HONEST AND TRUSTWORTHY

If you are not honest and trustworthy, earning the respect of your peers is nothing more than wishful thinking. People expect the truth, and they want to believe in the people for whom they work.

There are going to be times when you get difficult questions regarding your project or about the company running the project. Obviously, your crew will see you as the one who should be able to get to the bottom of their concerns. In order for your employees to feel connected to you as a leader, you need to prove to them that your intentions are genuine and that they can believe in what you say.

Foremen who beat around the bush instead of giving a straight answer are not doing themselves or their workers any favors. I would go so far as to say that some foremen actually get some kind of boost to their ego by having information that someone else needs or wants. Childish, self-serving behavior? Sure, yet it happens all the time.

Look at it this way. It doesn't matter who you are, if you dodge questions with ambiguous answers you will be viewed as deceptive. What you may see as being playful and coy is more than likely going to make your employees feel agitated and uncertain.

Uncertainty in the workplace breeds discontent.

Uncertainty in the workplace breeds discontent, which can spread through your crew without your ever knowing it. Ignore their requests a couple of times or make them feel as if you aren't shooting straight and at the very minimum you'll have a mental mutiny on your hands. When you come around they'll still be giving you the pleasantries you have come to expect from them, but on the inside, and with other coworkers, they'll care less about you and your success.

Disingenuousness and deceit will always be met with disdain.

LIKABILITY

Imagine how your work ethic and motivation might be compromised if every day you had to wake up knowing you were going to suffer through another shift working for a boss whom you hated, where every hour felt like four, where you spent long days dreaming of telling your foreman to go fly a kite, and where you wanted to quit in a blaze of glory and then land a new, more satisfying job. Maybe you woke up feeling that way today. Most folks can relate to this scenario because, let's face it, it's the way it is for many of us when we're working for someone in the position of authority who doesn't have the first clue about how to motivate, manage, or connect with people.

If you didn't wake up feeling this way, try to think about a time when you did. How hard is it to remember that one boss, that one particular name and face... Didn't a picture instantly pop into your head? We all have stories of the bad boss that stay clear in our minds because of the frustration and anger that comes with feeling trapped and unhappy.

Now take a moment to reflect on how the actions of this individual affected your performance and your mind set.

Remembering your own experience, why in the world would you give your employees (who are just like you were then) any reason not to like you? Do you really want to be the face that comes to mind when they're asked for the name of the most miserable foreman they ever worked for?

It doesn't matter how long you have been a foreman. It will always be difficult to maintain good employee relations while dealing with the compounding daily stress that comes along with every responsibility of your job. Just the pressure of worrying that your project is running efficiently and productively all day every day is enough to wear down your patience and put you on edge. Not only is it hard to have patience when you're stressed, but when your patience is depleted you have less ability to reason and make rational decisions. Soon, you become short with people and start jumping to conclusions when you don't think they're getting enough done.

CRACKING THE WHIP

For some foremen, their instinct tells them they should ratchet up the pressure on their crew and assert their power and authority by intimidating them to work harder. *This is a classic mistake!* Swinging your power over the heads of your crewmembers is never a good way to motivate them. Your crew are fully aware who the boss is.

They have seen your business card; they see where you park every day. There is no need to constantly remind them that you could send them packing at a moment's notice.

Cracking the whip and bird-dogging your crew might create an illusion in your own mind that you have everything in control, but it will be received by your crew as desperation and incompetence.

Are you thinking, "Why do I care if they like me? I'm not here to make friends. I'm here to get the job done." If this is your mind set, I will concede the point that you don't have to be "friends" with the people who work for you. On the other hand, you will always have more success—and get more from them—when your employees can find likable qualities in you that they believe to be genuine.

Workers in all industries work harder for the managers they like. It's the same for foremen.

Furthermore, if you are disliked you put yourself in the position of being taken advantage of. Your crew will find satisfaction in doing things behind your back to "even the score" because you've treated them poorly. The last thing you need when you are trying to run a successful project is to be the butt of every joke, the name most commonly seen on the bathroom wall, or the motivating factor behind the slacking off.

Remember, a crew of 10 can generate a high volume of wasted labor hours by slowing down simply for the sake of trying to punish you. It might be taking a long lunch break, failing to inform you that your supply of material is getting low, or just by paying less attention to detail as they complete their tasks. All it takes is a few minutes here and a few minutes there and before you know it an hour has been burned up without an iota of production.

You may hold a certain amount of power over the individuals on your crew, but they also hold a collective power over you. It's kind of like group therapy for your crew, who will find comfort in knowing others feel the same way they do. For you to ignore this fact is not only arrogant but foolish.

DO YOU CARE?

It has become apparent to me over the years that foremen with this approach are either truly unaware, don't care what people think (because they incorrectly surmise that being likeable has no bearing on the outcome of a project), or are so insecure and so controlling that they feel compelled to lead by fear and intimidation. Whatever the reason, discontent and an inferior project are the direct result.

We talked a bit earlier about how different it is when your crew is on your team. The benefits of being liked and admired are both many and meaningful. Not only will they tend to demonstrate compassion and willingness when the need arises, but they will do it even when you're not present to watch them. You need to have the willing eyes and ears of everyone on your crew focused on the pulse of the project.

On-the-Job Training: Telling the Truth

You are the foreman running a project, a 10-story building. You have a small crew on every floor, so there is no way you can spend enough time on each floor to spot all the coordination issues and material shortages or notice discrepancies in the blueprints. Every person on your crew has the potential to bring you pertinent information that allows you to spearhead a problem that you will otherwise be unaware and before it will cause a disruption in production.

Will someone on your crew feel compelled to share this vital information? How do you know?

The only way you can expect to receive this kind of help from your crew is if the individuals who work with you truly appreciate you and want to see you succeed. You can't have it both ways. To jump up and down screaming one minute and then ask for help the next doesn't work. Consistency sends your message every time.

One final thought about being "likeable" before we move on. Let's look at the easy analogy to our personal lives. How do you feel about the neighbor who is always willing to let you borrow a tool, jumps in to lend a hand whenever you're working on a project, and who happily keeps an eye on your place when you're gone on vacation? And how do you feel about the neighbor who never waves when he drives by, lets his dog use your front yard as a toilet, and whose hobby is playing drums to AC/DC songs at 3:00 in the morning?

Big difference, right? Now answer this: If both of your neighbors' cars were about to be towed, who would you call first? The first neighbor who's always around to help or the second neighbor with the impolite dog and the bad disposition?

If you're anything like me, I bet you'd call the friendly neighbor first. And perhaps sit and watch as the tow truck carts away the other neighbor's vehicle without lifting a finger.

This is exactly the way you need to look at your relationship with your crewmembers. Do you want them looking out for you or do you want them to look the other way and let you—or help you to—fail?

HOW TO BE THE TEACHER

One of the greatest rewards of learning a craft and developing expertise is being able to share your knowledge with others. One of the reasons I have enjoyed continuous and stable employment over the last 20 years, along with many opportunities to advance in my career, is due to the education I received as an apprentice and during my early days as a journeyman.

I was one of the fortunate ones. I started with a good company that employed talented craftsman who were always willing to teach me the tricks of the trade. These craftsmen continually tested my abilities and gave me as much responsibility as they thought I could handle. Over my five-year apprenticeship I gained a firm understanding of what it takes to make quality installations *and* maintain production expectations.

During this same five-year period I had many classmates who weren't so lucky, however. Some of them worked for contractors or journeymen who didn't see the true value that a well-trained apprentice could provide. Considering the fact that an apprentice only makes a percentage of a journeyman's wages, doesn't it stand to reason that an apprentice who can produce on a scale near that of a journeyman would be a huge benefit to the bottom line of a project?

I am not suggesting you want to have more than a few apprentices working on a project because they make a lower wage. You still need licensed and experienced professionals making decisions and carrying the bulk of the load. I am making the case, however, that an educated apprentice is a productive apprentice, and a productive apprentice is a valuable asset for any company.

On the other hand, if you choose to be circumspect about the information you share, telling an apprentice only the absolute minimum he needs to get by for the sake of maintaining control, you will probably regret it. It is only your paranoia telling you to worry that such an apprentice will someday show up to take your job away.

FINAL THOUGHTS

There is always going to be competition in the workplace, but I have found that my skills continually improve in the process of teaching someone else. Besides, a little competition is good for the psyche; it keeps us on our toes and forces us to grow. The truth is that those you teach will not be looking to knock you out of a job. If anything, they will become allies of yours in the years to come. These are the people who will be there to protect your best interests when you are not around. I know because every journeyman or foreman who helped me along the way will always be on the top of my list.

Chapter 21

Communication

When something goes wrong on a project and mistakes are made we all blame the "lack of communication." Since few people understand what it really means to be a good communicator, and therefore don't communicate their thoughts in a comprehensive way, I guess I'd have to agree. The surprising thing is that if you ask most foremen if they think they're good communicators, invariably they'll tell you they are. Try to get one of these foremen to explain what it means to be a good communicator, though, and you'll hear more hemming and hawing than anything else.

In my opinion, good communication is the ability to visually or verbally convey your thoughts to others and have those thoughts thoroughly comprehended.

Every single time I communicate with someone on my crew, it is my goal to walk away from the conversation feeling confident that the individual could now explain, in full detail, exactly what I just explained to him to another crewmember. When this happens, I know we have been communicating well and successfully.

GOOD COMMUNICATION

Communication is much more than speaking the words that describe the task you are giving an individual to do. Good communication is also confirming that this person completely hears, sees, and understands your vision. For this to happen, an exchange must take place that ensures you both understand each other's thoughts and conclusions.

For example, you might be explaining a project to a crewmember who is nodding his head and showing all the signs of understanding. But how can you be sure that what he's hearing is what you are trying to convey? It's important to recognize that nodding and agreeing are not necessarily true indicators that an understanding has been forged.

This section discusses many ways for you to increase the quality of the communication between you and your crew.

EFFECTIVE COMMUNICATION

We've established that you cannot control everything. The one thing you *can* control, however, is how well you communicate.

As discussed in the chapters on planning and organizing, one of your primary functions as a foreman is to transfer all the knowledge you have compiled about the project to your crew. All it takes is a few missed details in the passing of information and you could be looking at multiple mistakes, re-work, and/or loose ends.

Of course it is just as important that you receive good information from your crew about anything they might need or problems they foresee. Your ability to understand their questions and needs is as vital as the information you pass on to them.

That's why one of the best things you can do to promote good communication is to make it very clear to everyone on your crew that you place a high value on it. Let them know that no matter how small the question, how insignificant their concern may seem, you will always take the time to clarify anything that is unclear to them.

I really believe if more focus were put into training foremen to have great communication skills there would be far fewer misunderstandings and mistakes. What would that mean for your project? That's right, increased profits every time.

The following examples describe how to communicate effectively and how to educate your crewmembers to communicate more effectively with you. Reading these should help you see how easy it can be to think you are communicating well, when in fact you may be leaving important details to someone else's interpretation.

A poor communicator assumes the person receiving the information is more knowledgeable then he actually is.

---

1. As the foreman it's easy to forget that you are the only person within your entire crew who is constantly deciphering the blueprints in depth. This working knowledge of the project's many different facets is something

your crew, as a whole, will never possess. There are never enough labor hours in any project to have everyone on your crew spending large amounts of time scouring through the prints attempting to ingest every small detail. This is why your thorough understanding of the project is required. I would be willing to bet that in most cases even your most valuable workers in the field will spend only 5 to 10% of the time you spend studying the prints.

Throughout the early stages of the planning process and continuing through to the completion of the project you will unconsciously commit many details to your memory. Remain mindful of this fact when you are passing information on to your crew. If you don't, you may end up glossing over important details in an attempt to keep a conversation short.

2. As the responsible party your vigilance is required to assess the quality and content of all conversations as they relate to all installations on your project, whether you are explaining a task to someone on your crew or are having a conversation with another trade dealing with a coordination issue. Leaving any question unanswered or in limbo is unacceptable. *No matter the recipient of your communication, you must always provide clear and understandable explanations of your thoughts and demand the same in return.* The only possible exception to this is when you are absolutely positive the person has the same understanding about a task or issue as you do.

3. Recognize that some people feel anxious about asking too many questions. They want you to have faith in them and they never want to give you the impression that they don't know what they're doing. It's very easy to discourage someone from asking questions if you tease them or get short with them when they do ask.

In my view, you should be pleased when someone asks for clarification when something remains unclear. This clearly indicates that your employee or another foreman is interested in knowing as much as he can in order to make minimal mistakes, which equates to less wasted labor in the long run.

Foremen with good communication skills encourage their employees to ask questions as they are being given information about an upcoming task.

Foremen who emphasize good communication skills explain the task in multiple stages, stop at different points along the way to make sure the information being explained is understood, and periodically ask for questions from the crew.

Here is why this works so well. First of all, being able to ask questions along the way allows your crew to paint a more vivid picture in their mind as you take them through the various steps you want them to follow. Second, your employees may come up with a question about something you may have overlooked, which provides you with the opportunity to clear up any unknowns before work on a task has started.

Using this method ensures that you walk away from every conversation knowing there will be nothing left up to interpretation. This increases the accuracy of installations and eliminates unnecessary mistakes, a combination that accounts for a better labor/production rate for your project.

4. Let's go back for a minute to our foreman with the Superman complex (big ego). This type of foreman sees questions as a threat, rather than as an attempt to learn information. If he feels pushed into a corner or becomes embarrassed by being asked a question he believes he should know, he fabricates an answer that may be incorrect or makes the employee feel stupid for asking.

There are obvious pitfalls in reacting this way:

» If you choose to make up an answer on the fly to save face, you stand the chance of being incorrect. Once you take the time to investigate the question further, you may be forced to return to your employee to inform him that you gave him bad information. Is this any better than admitting you don't have the answer in the first place?

» If you make someone feel stupid for asking a legitimate question you will only discourage him from bringing up questions in the future. The thing to remember is that people are fully aware that you can't possibly memorize everything there is to know about a project. That's why your best bet is simply to say, "That's a good question. I'm not sure, let me do a little more research and I'll get back to you." Any other response and you're only fooling yourself and hurting the project.

5. Some foremen have the tendency to be or appear to be in too much of a hurry while passing information on to their crew. This form of poor communication sacrifices results for time—but only in the short run.

    You spend hours, days, or even weeks putting together a comprehensive and detailed plan for an upcoming task. You gather dimensions, establish an installation method, decide what material you will use, and coordinate with other trades. So, why at this critical juncture of explaining the task to your crew, at a time when the accuracy of information exchanged needs to be at its peak, would you attempt to dump all this information on them during the few minutes you have available before you head off to another meeting?

    Rushing off and cutting short explanations leaves your crew feeling they've gotten the short shrift. They don't have the chance to ask the questions they have or would have had if you had done a better job communicating the plan. They are left to interpret the details of the job based on uneducated guesswork.

    You are left with lots of wasted time and money.

Communicate in advance.

---

6. When you know someone on your crew will be moving to a new task in the near future, try to find a little extra time during the few days prior to starting the work to give him bits of information about what he will be doing next. A few well-placed details in advance will allow him to start thinking about the materials he may need or information that needs clarification. Then, when you are ready to start the project, it will actually start, not get hung up on necessary details.

There are never enough hours in the day and you'll always be in a rush to get things done. But time management issues can only be solved by you.

WHAT???

I've seen many foremen through the years rely on vague dialogue, hand gestures, and arm waves to communicate information. But these methods are poor substitutes for good layout. Saying things like, "You know, over by that column," or "Just do it the way we did it that one time," is begging for trouble. Sure, you'll get a head nod or two in response, but you'll have no idea if the individual really understood.

If you see these false signals as confidence, the problem will only be compounded. At the conclusion of all this miscommunication, your crew can easily walk away thinking they know exactly what and where, and you can walk away fully unaware they might be on the road to installing something incorrectly or in the wrong location. If maximum efficiency and production are the goal, you can't let this happen.

Vague communications also have the effect of making you appear unprofessional or uninformed or both, and slowly strip away your credibility with other trades, customers, crew, and supervisors. If the roles were reversed, wouldn't you want the foreman in charge to be convincingly competent, informed, and professional?

This level of professionalism should be the standard for all foremen. Your crew is counting on you for accurate information about installations. Your supervisor is counting on you to run the most efficient and productive job possible. And the customer needs to feel you are fully qualified to manage and build the job.

On-the-Job Training: "Do It Like That"

You are the foreman of a framing crew. You need one of your employees to frame in a column. Do you say, "Go over there and frame in that one column. Frame it like...you know, that one Joe framed on the third floor," and wave your arm in the general direction of the task?

Or do you describe the task in the simplest, most precise way to get the result you want? "I want you to frame column 5B. If you have any questions ask Joe. He framed one just like it on the third floor." Clearly, this is a much better start to achieving your objective.

Remember, you might be visualizing column 5B in your mind and the specifications detailing how it needs to be framed, but you can't be sure your crew sees the same vision. It doesn't cost more time or energy to communicate in a way that removes all confusion.

Because not everyone learns or communicates the same way (some are more visual and some more auditory), adding a print or a hand-drawn sketch again ratchets up the likelihood that your directives are followed and the installment is done according to specifications.

Communicating in a manner best suited to the individual is the kind of attention to detail that makes a good foreman great.

COMMUNICATION DOS AND DON'TS

Practicing the five skills listed below will put you on the right track to becoming a great communicator. I suggest you mark this page for future reference. If up to this point in your career communication has not been one of your strong suits, it may take time and a conscious effort for your habits to change. The good news is that they will. Once these guidelines become second nature your jobs will run more smoothly, mistakes and re-work will be minimized, and you will become a model example for others to follow.

1. Know the specifics of the project yourself. Preparation is the key. Leave nothing to chance. Do your research and try to anticipate any question or detail you might need for the installation. This first step is the most important because if you aren't able to explain a task thoroughly, you can't possibly expect that your crew will get the full picture.

2. Explain the project thoroughly to your crew from start to finish.

3. Answer any questions as they come up so every crew-member stays mentally present with you during the entire conversation. All it takes is one statement to be unclear for the rest of the conversation from that point forward to be lost. You may continue to talk about more details and directions, but those listening will be thinking back to the earlier part of your description that they did not fully understand and will thus miss even more valuable information.

4. What should you do when you think someone has a question, but he doesn't stop you to ask it? Look for clues. Use your intuition. Body language usually lets you know whether or not the crew is with you in mind and body or just in body. If at any time you sense you're losing someone, stop and clarify. You don't have to pick that person out from the crowd. Instead, say something like, "Remember, there are no stupid questions. Asking now before the project starts is the best way to do it right." You may give the questioner the impetus and the okay to speak up.

5. At the conclusion of the conversation be sure to encourage questions once again. Anyone reluctant should feel comfortable enough at this point to ask. Make a note of any questions for which you don't have answers and get back to the individuals who asked the questions.

6. Check back in with your crew. Don't wait too long to come back and check on your crew's progress. New ques-

tions are sure to arise during the first stages of the task and the answers may not be immediately available. This will give you a head start on finding those answers.

COMMUNICATION WITH OTHER TRADES

The importance of good communication between *every* trade cannot be overstated because it is key to each individual foreman's success. Projects end up in disarray when every trade is not on the same wavelength and in agreement on everything from scheduling to installations. This means establishing a common direction and realistic completion goals.

Think about what would happen if, instead of communicating first, the various trades on a project came rushing into the project with only their installations in mind. Wouldn't it end up more of a race to see who will get in first? When none of the trades are thinking about how their installation might affect anyone else, material piles up everywhere, the site becomes disorganized, schedules get missed, and tensions run high. Sometimes fights are known to break out.

To avoid this kind of scenario, follow your well-conceived plan with good communication and follow through on your commitments. One trade that falls behind schedule impacts all of the other trades on the job, so if you do find yourself falling a little behind schedule let the other trades know about it as soon as you realize a problem exists.

It's not uncommon for there to be kinks in every plan, given the fact that there are so many variables or moving pieces in every project. That's why it's so important to be flexible and to make the honest effort of letting the others know where the problem is. This way they'll have enough time to make provisions for their crew(s) to work somewhere else. Just as you are scheduling and planning the direction your crew is heading, the other trades are doing the same for their crews, and as far in advance as they can.

Foremen use the schedules and completion dates of the other trades to build their own schedules. When you are up front and honest, people are willing to work with you because they can relate to your circumstances. If you form a habit of waiting until the last minute, however, you will certainly frustrate the other foremen, who will then be less inclined to help you in the future.

SEE NO EVIL

Oh, and one last thing: Blinders don't work. Walking around with blinders on so that you can ignore the needs of other trades makes it virtually impossible to meet your completion goals. It is that cut and dry. Cooperation is absolutely essential, and there is no debating it. Only a group effort will make your job a success.

There have always been, and always will be, a percentage of foremen who believe their installations should take precedence over those of the other trades. I have been witness to this kind of short-sighted thinking, which creates a tension-filled working environment and discontentment for every foreman on a project. You know how it is...all it takes is one bad apple. If a foreman like this is present on one of your projects, stand together with the remaining foremen who understand the value of good communication and cooperation to keep the one bad seed from affecting the success of the project for everyone.

FINAL THOUGHTS

Over your career working on multiple job sites and applying your craft, you have learned new ways of doing things that have made your job easier and increased your production. The tools you carry in your bag now probably look different from the tools you showed up with on your very first day of work as an apprentice or laborer, and you've likely made adjustments that have led you to be a productive member of your crew.

Now, to become a successful foreman, you have one additional tool to adopt and carry with you at all times: good communication skills.

Chapter 22

Motivation

Hunger motivates us to find food; thirst sends us in search of hydration. These are two simple examples of internal motivators that are derived from unconscious survival instincts that we all have as humans. In this discussion about motivation in relation to being a foreman in the construction industry, I ask you to see motivation as a supplement to the work ethic and drive each individual brings to your project. Any inducement you provide will only add to this innate factor.

Inspiring your crew has many benefits. First, it helps create reliable employees who come to work every day ready to tackle the day's challenges. Second, it encourages every individual to take personal pride and ownership in his part of a successful project. Third, since your ultimate goal as a foreman is to have skilled and enthusiastic employees who push themselves to excel because they want to, not out of fear of being fired, you will create an environment of competence and responsibility.

DEVELOPING YOUR OWN INSPIRATIONAL STYLE

To become an accomplished leader you need to discover your own brand of inspiration because your personal leadership style will dictate how you use motivation to reach your production goals. First, recognize that no two people react the same way to motivational methods. Second, there are plenty of motivational techniques that *never* work on anyone. Third, every project will require a different approach. Not only will the landscape and building design change, but so will the members on your crew. What works to motivate your crew on one project can fail dismally under different conditions in the next. This means a constant reevaluation and readjustment of your approach.

We are already clear on the fact that motivation is never accomplished through intimidation, threats, or condescending dialogue. We are also clear that this type of "incentive" is generally only used by foremen who are either in over their heads or who lack the people skills described earlier.

Threatening and intimidating your employees makes you an adversary, and adversaries don't inspire loyalty or the hard work necessary to complete a project successfully.

I have never heard anyone say that he enjoyed working for a company or a foreman where he felt his job was threatened every single day. What I have heard more times than I can count are complaints about foremen who continually treat their crews poorly.

Venting can take place anywhere: in the lunch trailer, out on the job site, walking in or out of work. I've even received phone calls at home from coworkers who are frustrated and angry about the foreman on the project. Meanwhile, the foreman is none the wiser to the dissent. People might tolerate the antics of a foreman with poor leadership skills for a while, but trust me when I tell you that every single employee of a tyrant has one foot out the door and is constantly in search for a better opportunity.

Working for a foreman who has great technical skills but lacks leadership skills is frustrating and discouraging. The employee is left to wonder if the foreman doesn't care, is not capable of communicating, or is simply misguided.

You can't afford to let yourself become so one-dimensional in your approach that you lose sight of the goal.

You can't be an effective leader if everyone who works for you thinks you can't hack it.

"IT'S THEIR FAULT"

Doesn't it make sense that the people working for you should want to be there and not feel as if a gun is being held to their head? Some foremen hold the false belief that people are either motivated on their own or not. They don't believe there is anything they can do to increase motivation and boost crew morale.

These foremen will tell you that most construction workers fall into one of three categories (or a combination of all three): independent, cocky, and/or disconnected. The truth is that although some people who work for you will have one or more of those characteristics, their personalities have very little to do with your ability to motivate your crew.

That's right. It is *always* possible to motivate your crew. Once you add some concrete motivational methods to your arsenal of skills, not only will your job become easier and more rewarding, but motivating others will become a natural part of who you are as a leader. You'll know you you've reached this point when you start to motivate others without consciously making the effort.

In construction, there are many jobs available and many different contractors offering work. If or when pushed, any craftsman with exemplary skills will have no problem finding a company where he feels appreciated. Companies who understand their success is hinged on employing individuals who are reliable, trustworthy, and skilled in their trade are always in search of quality individuals who have been forced to leave competitors due to unruly foremen and poor working conditions.

A successful foreman surrounds himself with competent individuals who complement his own skills and abilities. If you have the best people with the highest skills on your crew, you have an advantage many foremen will never have the luxury of enjoying.

Why would anyone continue to work for a foreman who belittles him and doesn't treat him with respect, especially when he knows he has a choice?

When you treat people poorly, your options for building a crew that regularly exceeds expectations become nonexistent. You are left to employ the individuals other foremen or contractors don't want. How will your chances for success be now?

MOTIVATIONAL METHODS

Earlier we talked about the fact that there are many different techniques for motivating people. I have been on the receiving end of some and have implemented plenty of others throughout my career with varying success. I share some of them with you here with explanations of why I believe they can work or why they fall short of the intended outcome.

1. *Offering a prize at the end of a predetermined amount of time.* Offering rewards based on the completion of the current phase of a project, on production and performance, or on the accomplishment of a set amount of labor hours without a loss-time injury sounds like a good idea, but usually fails to motivate a change in work habits. Don't get me wrong, anything you or your company do to show your appreciation for a job well done is good, but I am of the belief that this method is overrated in its motivational value.

   Motivation and appreciation are part of an ongoing process that requires ongoing work, not a carrot at the end of a stick. Addressing your crew every couple of months isn't effective. Again, I am not discouraging you from showing appreciation for your crew, but would like you to understand the difference between connecting with people on a personal level and congratulating the entire job site on a job well done.

One way to show appreciation is the pizza feed. (Any food is fine as long as it can be served as a free on-site meal; pizza is easy and the most common.) Every once in a while you can decide it's time to show your appreciation for your crew by buying a stack of pizzas for lunch on a Friday. But the reality is that while the crew will be pleased to chow down on the pizza—after all, it's a free meal—you can be sure you will not have influenced anyone to do anything above and beyond what they would normally do. They may line up like a pack of wolves licking their chops, but the feeling of appreciation only lasts until lunch is over. Then it's back to business as usual.

2. *Giving away T-shirts, hats, and coffee mugs.* Companies believe that handing out company promotional products is a show of appreciation that will be received in the spirit with which they are given. I personally believe that workers do appreciate the gesture and that it does help build loyalty, but like the pizza, if it's free anyone will line up for it. Just because a worker has a coffee mug in his hand doesn't mean that he will turn around and go back to work with a sudden renewed passion for the company's success. Handouts don't build trust and loyalty the way words and actions can.

In both these cases, any motivational success gained is generally short-lived. This is partly because whether it's pizza or a mug, it comes in the hand of someone from upper-level management who suddenly arrives on site to tell everyone what a great job they're doing. As someone who has spent many years working in the field, I can honestly say that I never felt someone I'd only met a few times (if ever) who didn't know me personally or what I meant to the project was capable of accurately making that judgment. The only person qualified to judge my work was my foreman.

Sure, the foreman can pass information up to management, but the usual standard accolades feel superficial in this kind of a group setting. Plus, those of us who are working on the project find ourselves suddenly being addressed by what equates to a stranger in shiny shoes, khaki pants, and a button-down shirt, while we sit there in our grubby work clothes. Even if it's only perceived as such by the workforce, the impression is that there is a level of disconnect between both parties.

3. Furthermore, it's possible that your best employees may resent the fact that you and your supervisor have lumped everyone into the same category. On every project I have ever worked there has been a wide disparity of skill and productivity levels. That's why I believe that it's always better to recognize individuals who are carrying more than their fair share of weight in contributing to the project. When you connect on the individual level you will find that the group's motivation level rises as well.

CONNECTING

During your daily or weekly communication with your supervisor, let him know who on your crew is doing an exceptional job. Bear in mind that there is no need to put down other employees in the process. Share the fact that there are a few individuals you'd like to recognize. Your supervisor can then take the initiative while on site to visit these employees where they're working and express his appreciation personally. Thanking an employee face to face is much more effective than thanking everyone as a group as described above.

Good motivators understand something that the others don't. They know that employees who feel valuable, involved, and appreciated 40 hours a week are much more likely to be productive and have good morale. They understand that sprinkling a little appreciation around here and there doesn't get the same results. It seems so obvious to me, yet many foremen don't recognize the value of consistent appreciation, or perhaps they can't muster up the energy to make it happen.

Make sure your employees know you are counting on them and that you can't do your job without them. Build on this approach every day. A crew that appreciates that you are genuine in your approach and aren't simply seeking glory will want to help you succeed.

NEGATIVE FEEDBACK

While we are on the subject, let's talk about the tough job of giving criticism. You can call it negative feedback or critical input or anything else you want, but there are many foremen who are uncomfortable providing it to crewmembers who aren't pulling their weight. I can understand their reticence. It's never easy to tell someone he's not doing a good job. But if you lie or embellish or omit or avoid while expressing to an employee what you think about his production or value, you'll regret it for sure.

First, if you aren't honest with someone you feel could be more productive you are setting a standard in his mind that is below your true expectations. Second, people know when their foreman is blowing smoke. Not only is it insulting, but it doesn't gain you any respect. So, be honest. When someone needs to work on his production let him know about it, offer some ideas about how to improve, and then do what you can to help him achieve his goals.

The longer you work with an individual the more opportunities you will have to build a wealth of knowledge about him that will assist you in communicating with him and motivating him. Knowing about his family life, hobbies, and especially his work habits will undoubtedly give you a better understanding about who he really is.

Since most people exhibit different personas at work than they do at home with friends and family, it always helps to try to get to know them a little. Many of my working relationships have benefitted by knowing the individuals on a more personal level. I'm not saying you have to invite them over to dinner, but if you take some time to ask them about their family lives and interests you may be able to expand the parameters of your working relationship and the project.

On-the-job Training: "My Way or the Highway"

You are the foreman on a project. You have an employee who is usually prompt, makes accurate installations, and has a good work ethic. At some point you begin to notice he is making mistakes, taking longer than usual to complete tasks, and generally appears to be out of sorts. Because you're of the "my way or the highway" and the "your paycheck should be enough motivation" mentality, before long you find yourself telling him if he doesn't kick it into high gear you're going to send him packing. A week later he's gone.

"Good riddance," you say, and wash your hands of the matter.

How is this approach flawed? First, you can't always be in the precise location where your employees are working. That means you have no way of knowing why production might be lacking. You've made a snap judgment based on your assumption about a situation without really knowing any of the facts. This approach means being wrong more times than not.

Second, if you assume the only reason this employee is not completing a task on your time schedule is because he is slacking off, you are not only exhibiting the habits of a poor motivator, but you are also being unfair to the individual. For all you know, this worker's poor production may be caused by not having the tools or materials he needs for the project. Maybe it's difficult to get the work done because the area where he's working is congested with other trades.

There are always legitimate reasons for production to be less than it should be. The responsibility lies squarely on your shoulders to make sure there are no obstacles hampering your crewmember's performance—and to find out the true nature of the employee's disappointing production.

Third, your haste to judgment can cause collateral damage. When the rest of your crew finds out how you handled the situation (and they will), they could start to see you as an intimidator who jumps to conclusions. This is no way to build respect, trust, and loyalty from your crew.

If you are truly dedicated to motivating your crew, you need to take the time to collaborate with them to find solutions to challenges *before* making your mind up about what you believe to be true. Remember, every time you help an individual learn a new way to do something or work with them to solve a problem you increase the value they contribute to your highly skilled team.

But what if you were to do things differently? Remember, your usually prompt employee, the one who makes accurate installations and has a good work ethic, has been making mistakes, taking longer than usual to complete tasks, and has seemed out of sorts.

This time, recalling the motivational tools at your disposal, you decide to have a private conversation with the employee to try and find out why he is struggling with productivity and meeting his deadlines. Because you have built trust and mutual respect with this employee, you don't have any problem talking with him about what is affecting his work. In this case, you find out something outside the work site is affecting his frame of mind. Because you value him as an employee, you try to help him with his problem, partly by giving him a little leeway while he works things out.

By approaching the individual with concern instead of a tirade about production you have let him know that you want to help. What better way is there to earn loyalty and respect?

On-the-Job Training: Disappointing Results

On this project you are the foreman of a crew of 15. Two of those individuals consistently fail to get done what you expect from them. What do you do?

As you did with your struggling employee above (and because it worked so well), you again try the conversational approach. You ask these two individuals if there is anything you can do for them that will increase their production. Unfortunately, this time no inroads are made and the employees continue to fall far short of your fair expectation.

At this point it may be fair to say there is a lack of desire to produce on the part of these two individuals. What do you do?

Many of us might decide to spend a little more time checking up on these employees, tiptoeing around to look over their shoulders in order to get the scoop, perhaps catch them in the act—whatever that act is. But such an approach usually backfires. Taking on the role of a snoop means looking at everyone on the crew with a microscope. In the process of trying to figure out what's going on with two individuals, suddenly we're spying everyone to discover their "secrets."

You know as well as I do that if there is one thing that shuts people down it's a foreman who assumes that because one person is slacking off the rest of the crew is slacking off, too.

I think I'm like most people in that I don't appreciate being heaped in with slackers who work with me on a project. When a foreman or upper management team threatens the entire crew rather than focusing on the few people who are the problem, it only makes me resentful. Do they think I need to sit through a reprimand I don't have coming? Do they think that when I walk out of a meeting where I felt attacked that I will be excited to get back to work...to be as productive as I can?

It has always been my contention that if indeed my foreman really saw me in the same light as the "problem" individuals then it was probably time to be working for someone else who knew the difference.

Oh, and don't forget that spying can lead to paranoia and that the path of paranoia is one you do not want to travel. There are always other solutions to a production problem, whether it's due to one individual or many.

Here are a few tips:

1. *Deal only with the individual or individuals who are not producing.* Be very direct and make it clear to them that you want to work with them, but also that if they can't find a way to produce at the level of everyone else you will have no choice but to let them go. This is a fair approach that gives them the opportunity to make the requested adjustments. Most people will respond by working to improve their behavior; the ones who don't should be terminated.

A person with a bad attitude can poison the morale of your entire crew. Deal with them as soon as you detect a problem.

---

2. *Don't waste one of your most valuable resources: time.* When you are consumed and frustrated by a couple of individuals, every minute you spend worrying they aren't doing what they are supposed to be doing added to the time you spend lurking around the job site trying to catch them in some act, you aren't doing what you need to be doing...planning and organizing for upcoming phases of your project.

Recognize that most people are honest, hardworking, and willing and ready to put in a hard day's work for you. When you get caught up in the pressures of your responsibilities, schedules, and expectations it can be easy to get trapped in the mind set that everyone is looking for a free ride and that everyone's intentions are suspect. But this kind of negative outlook can take over your common sense.

The fact is that the majority of people show up every day with the intention of doing a good job. It is your job to make sure they can do it.

Here are my four simple rules for motivating on the job site. If you are genuine in your approach, have reasonable production expectations, and encourage individuals to excel at their trade, you will have no problem forming high caliber teams that can accomplish any challenge you set out for them.

1. *Trust people.* People who feel trusted feel empowered. On the flip side, they'll take it personally if you don't trust them. Give them the benefit of the doubt until they prove themselves to be untrustworthy.

2. *Pay compliments when they're due.* Nothing goes further to motivate individuals than a genuine compliment from you, their foreman, especially when it's in the presence of their peers or another supervisor. People are proud of the work they do and feel appreciated when a supervisor acknowledges their efforts. Because some individuals will be embarrassed by this kind of attention, try not to make them uncomfortable with too much attention. And don't forget to be sincere. Lavishing unwarranted praise only spawns resentment.

3. *Give credit for good work.* Always give credit where and when it's due for the accomplishments of the individuals who made them happen. Most construction professionals spend many years learning and perfecting their crafts. Never jump in to take the credit for someone else, especially when a supervisor, another trade, or the customer is there to take notice.

4. *Show appreciation.* Saying a simple "thank you" or "great job today" goes a mile toward keeping an individual feeling engaged and motivated. The outcome is well worth any conscious effort you make.

FINAL THOUGHTS

What we've discussed here are simple solutions to common problems. The great thing is that applying them won't cost your company any money and doesn't require unreasonable amounts of time. The best part is that a committed and hardworking crew will be your reward.

Chapter 23

Crew Morale

Motivation and morale are close cousins and both impact the overall success of your project. Motivation is your first priority because your success sets the tone for the morale of the entire crew. Lack of motivation and indifference, whether about you or the project, affects every other member of your crew.

A CREW THAT WORKS TOGETHER TALKS TOGETHER

Think about how much time your crew spends together when you're not around. Think about the conversations they're having while they're working, on break, eating lunch, or having a beer after work. All it takes is for two or more of your crewmembers to show up at a gang box at the same time looking for material or tools that aren't there for the first signs of trouble to appear...a couple of people commiserating about how ironic it is that the foreman has high production expectations, but doesn't give them what they need.

That's all it takes to get the bad morale snowball rolling. And as the snowball rolls down the hill and out of control and gets bigger and bigger more people and more frustrations get drawn into the conversation. Soon you are the foreman who doesn't care and is in over your head, and it'll take a lot of effort to prove otherwise.

Never be so naïve or full of yourself to think your crew will be above discussing your shortcomings. It's just another facet of human nature to seek out validation for our frustrations when we're not satisfied with our job or the way we're being treated. That's why I always advise focusing first on the individual. Once you have established mutual respect with each member of your crew, motivating the crew as a whole should be a piece of cake.

"I KNEW HIM WHEN..."

If you are lucky enough to have a successful history with individuals who have worked with you before and who are now working with you on a current project, you will find them to be important assets. As the crew grows in numbers these people often help stamp out any signs of bad morale before it gains traction. These are the people who advocate for you when you aren't around and bring you issues from the field that need addressing. Their presence and support gives you the advantage of taking care of problems before they become a point of contention between you and your crew.

Crew morale should never be undervalued relative to its effect on the success of any project you ever run.

We know how success and profits in the construction industry are directly correlated to production. So, it only stands to reason then that if the people who have the power to increase or decrease production are content, engaged, and motivated, your success and longevity as a foreman (and your chance of running a successful project) will remain intact.

There is also no doubt that keeping your crew upbeat and involved in the process will pay you long-term dividends throughout your career.

MORALE BUSTERS

I could write another entire book about what brings morale down, but that is not my objective. Instead I have chosen to provide information and tools to help foremen become great leaders.

I have come to believe that the best way to get the message across is to describe typical situations that can be regarded from the perspective of a crew; in other words, from the perspective of the people who work for you, the foreman. This approach should help you gain understanding about what causes frustration and how frustration often leads to widespread dissatisfaction. These morale-busting examples come from my personal experiences in the construction industry and should shed some light on the challenges every foreman faces.

> *Moral buster #1: Missing tools and materials.* I've said it before, but it can't be said too often because this is a common theme in the industry. The majority of people show up to work every day with the intent of putting in a good day's work. If you don't keep the job stocked with tools and material you have effectively removed their opportunity to be efficient and productive before they have ever gotten started. Soon

your crew will have lost interest in your success and the project.

Going hand in glove with disinterest is a general lack of drive and desire to perform. From your crew's perspective, if it appears you don't seem to care if they are efficient they will simply follow your "lead" and slow down.

Are they wrong in their thinking? If your response is, "That's absurd, of course I want them to be efficient and productive!" then make a note here. Your actions always speak louder than your words. No matter what you say it is the example you set that matters.

On-the-Job Training: No Blueprints

You show up for work on your first day as a foreman. Your supervisor tells you to "get out there on site and start developing a plan." You want to do what he's telling you to do, but he hasn't given you a set of blueprints. What do you do?

Most people in this situation would look the supervisor right in the eye and say, "What exactly do you expect me to do if I don't even know what I'm going to be building?" Yes, you have the option of traveling the site to try to find out about the project from another trade, but you can be sure that approach won't give you or your company much credibility as professionals.

Now look at this through your crew's eyes. How can you expect them to maintain the highest possible levels of efficiency and production if you don't provide them with all the tools, material, and information they need? Answer: you can't.

On-the-job Training: "Go Borrow It"

You are a journeyman on a project. Every time you need a tool or materials you don't have, your foreman tells you, "Go borrow it from someone else." How do you feel?

Although there will be times when borrowing from another trade might be necessary, and it is crucial that trades work together in a crunch, using this approach habitually becomes a crutch. As such it is used by those foremen who don't plan well.

I believe that a foreman should never have his crew do his dirty work. If you have to ask for favors from another contractor, do it yourself. That is your job. As the project leader, it is up to you to establish relationships with the foremen from every other trade.

Early on in any project the foremen should come together as a group to arrive at an understanding about what they are willing to do for each other. To send an employee off to borrow or hijack tools or materials from another contractor is an attempt to skirt one of the core responsibilities of being a foreman, and puts him in an awkward position. Don't forget, if the other foreman has the tools or material it's because he has properly planned for his crew's needs.

This last point about having what your crew needs is more closely related to production than morale, but it affects both. Every time you borrow a tool, a ladder, a lift, or any other equipment from another contractor you have to hope his crew won't need it while your crew is using it. If that contractor has to come and take it back because his crew now needs it, the hours will begin to add up relative to time lost based on your poor planning.

Let's consider this event in more detail. First, there is lost time when your employee looks for the tool he is never going to find because you haven't made it available. Second, there is lost time while your employee takes the time to find you and tell you he doesn't have what he needs to complete his project. Third, there is lost time when your employee searches the project for another contractor who has what he needs so he can ask to borrow it.

We can even throw in yet another variable that costs even more wasted labor. Suppose the contractor comes back and takes the borrowed item because his crew needs it before your crewmember is finished. Now your employee has to stop what he is doing again and again start the process of finding another tool to borrow.

Wouldn't you agree that this is an ill-conceived strategy for running an efficient project?

Do not take this problem lightly. Keep in mind that this example affects only one employee one time. To get the true picture you'd have to multiply the damaging results by the number of employees you have by the number of instances when this situation occurs. The impact on the profitability of your project can be huge. Depending on the size of your crew you can lose anywhere from an hour a day to many hours a day due to preventable unproductive down time.

Step into the shoes of your company's owner and try to swallow that one.

But let's get back to why the lack of proper tools and material drives down morale. When you aren't around to see what's going on, your whole crew is likely complaining—or even arguing with each other—about not having what they need. As you go about your day, you have no idea how your poor planning and execution is grinding down your crew's morale.

In the meantime, resentment toward you and other coworkers continues to build because you are not providing them with what they need. Unwittingly, you have created a crew of people who end up working against each other.

I have seen this happen many times and believe me when I say it can get ugly. Some people start hiding tools because they know they're going to need them again soon and want to be able to find them. Others start sneaking around and taking tools out of other people's work area when they're not around.

Do you want your crew to act like this?

Your crew knows success is directly tied to production the same way you do. These are people who are in direct competition with each other for their jobs. They know they are responsible for being productive. They know when it comes time to evaluate their performance you are going to use their production as part of the equation. If you are the type of foreman who repeatedly asks for the impossible or doesn't give your crew what they need, you have stacked the deck against them.

Typically this kind of foreman doesn't want to hear any excuses, legitimate or otherwise. He especially doesn't want to hear if the reasons have anything to do with the fact that he is not doing his job. In this case, each crewmember is left to individually fend for himself, to attempt to accomplish what he can, even if it means causing dissention with the rest of the crew. This kind of devastating result could easily have been avoided if the foreman utilized good communication skills and proper planning techniques.

Morale buster #2: Alienation. Without the recognition they deserve and need, your crew will feel alienated from you and their work. Plus, if the crew is not getting their due in terms of well-deserved recognition, one can only assume that you are taking credit for all their hard work! This is both self-serving and extremely damaging to your perceived character as a leader.

Great leaders put aside their own need for recognition and focus on the needs of their crew. Too many times I have seen foremen take the position that since they aren't receiving credit from their supervisors, they don't need to recognize and compliment the people who work directly for them.

This harmful and immature approach hurts everyone. Although the job cannot be completed without you or your crew, you are the one in the position to make sure your crew gets the credit they deserve when they do a good job. Don't redirect your frustrations about something that is not your crew's fault onto them. If you have a problem with the people you work for, take it up with them and leave your crew out of it.

Morale Buster #3: Work-site politics. Politics exist on every job site, but involving your crew in the conflicts that arise among the other trades on a project or with your own supervisor is sure to bring down everyone's spirits. These things don't need to be part of your conversations with your crew and can cause other types of dissention. For example, let's say you are having a disagreement with the foreman of another trade and you express your feelings to your crew. The next thing you know they're inciting problems out in the field with the other trade's foreman and crewmembers. Why? Out of loyalty for you.

Getting your employees involved only exacerbates the problem, and all the contractors on the project will suffer from the larger consequences. Discuss all conflicts and issues directly with your supervisor or the foreman of the other trade to resolve it quickly. Keep your employees focused on the tasks they have been given and you will keep the project moving forward.

I'm going to share something that happened to me a few years ago as I was about to start a new project. The experience could easily have caused me to have a bad attitude before I ever stepped foot on the project and had the opportunity to get my tools out and get to work. Fortunately, however, by this time in my career I had begun to think about the importance of communication, motivation, and crew morale and their effects on the success of a project, and was therefore able to look at the situation a little bit more objectively than I might have in prior years.

Before I share the details, I have to admit that the foreman on this project took me by surprise. In fact, his behavior and the tactic he used to communicate his expectations was shocking to me. I can only imagine that it was an attempt to lessen his responsibility as it applied to the actions of his crewmembers. But because the people on his crew felt belittled and disrespected, it backfired. You can judge for yourself.

At the time I joined this project it was already in high gear. I was going to be working for a foreman I had known for a long time, but I had only worked with him when we were both apprentices. We had never worked together as journeymen and neither of us had ever run a crew that the other had worked on. I had no expectations either way as to whether this individual would be a good foreman to work for.

The first day I walked into his trailer to find out the particulars of what I was going to be doing, the foreman said a brief hello and then handed me a piece of paper. This paper listed all his "rules and regulations" for the project.

Now, I understand that it's easier to write a few key items on a piece of paper so employees have something to reference if they need it while they work. You know, helpful things like times to take a break and have lunch, the foreman's contact information, and emergency numbers and procedures should there be an accident...The kind of things most people appreciate having and that make sense in terms of making sure everyone has the same information.

But this list went way beyond common sense.

The foreman had handed me a list that covered the entire front and back of an 8.5 x 11 page. The list was single spaced and in such a small print that it was almost impossible to read. Immediately I became suspect of this foreman's intentions. Was he trying to insult me? Was he lumping me into his entire crew, assuming—suggesting—I could not handle myself professionally on his site? Frankly, I was boiling.

At the time of this experience, I was nearly 40 years old and had 20 years in the trade. As you know, I started in the construction industry when I was 16 as a material handler. My father was an electrician and an electrical contractor, and I worked summers with him during high school and after I graduated. I completed a five-year apprenticeship to become a licensed electrician. I ran my first job as a foreman when I was only out of my apprenticeship for a month, and that was 10 years before walking onto this job. Not to mention the fact that I had been a foreman on many projects since. None of that seemed to matter.

It amazes me even now that although this foreman knew everything about me, including my work ethic, my skills, and my on-the-job experience, he still insisted on having me read his "rules and regulations," and then sign a sheet acknowledging I had read it.

Dumbfounded, I did what he asked. I stood in the trailer and read the list...but what was really going on in my head was that I had never been treated with such a lack of respect or acknowledgment for my skills and professionalism in all the years I'd been working in the industry.

To be fair, we'll take a minute to review a couple of rules from this foreman's list of rules and regulations. I hope my comments about it will give you some insight into why such a method does not work as a good communication tool and how it contributes to bad morale.

The first rule I remember reading was, "Use a level whenever running conduit." I probably don't have to tell you that telling an electrician to use a level is like telling a carpenter which way the nail should be facing when he hammers two boards together. This request (demand) was unnecessary given my skill level, demonstrated a general lack of trust on the foreman's part, and made me feel like "just another worker" on his project.

The second rule, "Tighten all couplings, connectors, and straps," had the same effect. Again, unless the person working for you is a brand new apprentice or you know him from a prior experience and feel the need to impart these basic instructions, employing this level of direction is demeaning at best. I know I interpreted this foreman's approach to mean that he expected the worst from everyone, but from me in particular.

If you remember, the first rule of motivation is to trust the people with whom you work. Until someone proves to be untrustworthy or you determine they lack certain skills, it's best to give him the benefit of the doubt. Of course this only applies if you are truly trying to earn his respect and motivating him to do their best. If you treat him with disdain you can be sure of two things: he won't respect you and he won't trust you.

Does it sound as if I was a little too sensitive? That I overreacted to this foreman's method of communication? Perhaps I was and did, but I was definitely not the only person who had a problem with this list. In fact, the foreman's list was a constant topic of conversation out in the field—and it wasn't because anyone thought it was a good idea. The foreman's list had become a joke, where every time one worker walked by another he'd shout, "Hey, are you using your level? Did you make sure to tighten your couplings?" The list that the foreman believed was so helpful in getting his crew to do what he wanted had become a tool for mocking him instead.

Some time has passed since that project was completed, but those of us who were there still get chuckle out of "The List." The foreman, believe it or not, still runs work, and will likely never know how the people who work for him perceive his leadership skills. Given his approach, it would be highly unlikely that anyone would feel emboldened enough to speak to him about his lack of skill or let him know how his list is being received. If someone did have the nerve to tell him about his morale busting list, you can be sure he'd assume it was one person's opinion, discard it as such, and do nothing to change it.

The bad news for a foreman with such a poor sense of interpersonal skills combined with a big ego is that his inability to use constructive criticism as a learning tool will only contribute to his lack of overall success and opportunity.

MORALE BOOSTING

Before we move on, I want to give you some of the best, tried and true ways to encourage and empower your crew to do a great job and get the results you desire. Naturally, they start with mutual respect and end with good communication.

On-the-Job Training: High Quality

You are the foreman of a project that demands a high-quality installation. The customer has expressed the desire to have a building they can be proud of for years to come. How do you address your crew?

Are you thinking that it would be a good idea to approach your crew in the morning before they go to work or after their lunch break for a conversation? Good, because you'd be right.

Are you thinking it could go something like this? "First of all, I want to tell all of you that you're doing a great job and the customer is very happy. Your work looks great and I appreciate everyone's efforts. Now that we are gearing up to start running conduit, I want to ask that you all continue to take great care in making a professional installation. This is an important customer to our company and they expect the best from us. Let's continue to show them what we are capable of. Thanks for your help, and keep up the good work."

Good! Then you'd be right again!

A few words like this take about 30 seconds to impart, and there is little chance your crew will find any part of your request to mock or to be worthy of complaint. Addressing the entire crew in this positive manner is not only a good way to get the results you are shooting for, but it is also an excellent way to earn their respect.

MORALE AND LEADERSHIP

With time and experience you will develop your own leadership style and ways to motivate your crew and build crew morale. There is no perfect recipe for you to follow line by line that will boost morale. Project variables and changing crew dynamics make it impossible to carry over exactly what worked on one project to the next. With that said, there are some things you can do to maintain and improve morale.

For example, I have never met anyone who didn't find it rewarding to be part of a winning team. Those people who work hard, get along well, feel like a valuable part of a team, and who have fun during the process find their jobs more gratifying. No one wants his job to be a miserable and unbearable grind. Being the foreman or part of a crew that is known to tackle the toughest projects successfully inspires feelings of ownership, pride, and motivation to continue giving your best.

If you do find yourself in the position of being part of a crew on a project that is unorganized, losing money, and constantly under fire from management, you can expect morale to be in bad shape as well. If you are the one running the crew, you need to step in at the onset to promote a winning attitude.

Some jobs are destined to be difficult. Some projects are bid incorrectly, which makes the prospect of making a profit unlikely. When you are asked to run such a project it is in your best interest to keep your crew focused, engaged, and upbeat.

Look at it this way. If your company takes on a project where it expects to lose 3% due to mistakes in the bidding process and you are able to finish the project with no loss at all, it will still be considered a positive outcome. That's why you can't walk around the job site hanging your head and spreading a pessimistic attitude to your crew.

Another way to boost morale is by keeping the crew informed about the status of the job and how you think the project is progressing. All this takes is a couple of minutes every few days or once a week. Let your crew know where the job is headed and how you see them working into your plans. They all want to feel as if they have some job security, and, in this case, you are the only one who can give it to them.

Think about what you like to receive from your supervisors. Isn't job security one of them? The best method for determining what will improve morale and keep individuals engaged is to turn things around and think about what would improve your morale if you were in your crew's position.

WHO STAYS AND WHO GOES

One of the most difficult tasks for any foreman is determining who will stay and who will be let go when it comes time to cut back his crew's size. As the end of the job draws near, it is common for the morale of the crew to start to slip. Everyone gets nervous about whether he will have another job waiting or whether he'll be one of the ones cut loose.

When you work in construction you are well aware that projects have a beginning and an end, but this fact doesn't change the anxiety that comes with the prospect of not having a job in the upcoming weeks. Over the years I have seen foremen prefer to blindside individuals rather than give them a little advance notice before they let them go. I don't see how anything good can be garnered by this kind of behavior.

At some point in my career it came to my attention that some foremen believed that if they gave any advance notice then the individual would simply shut down and any reasonable amount of production would cease. I myself don't buy in to this paranoid and destructive way of thinking.

First of all, if an individual has done a good job for you, I think he is owed the common courtesy of being informed about your plans. Plus, even if you treated the person well while he was on your job, if you let him go without warning that will be the last thing he'll remember about you. Do you want to send someone away from your project thinking you lack compassion and respect for him as an individual or would you rather he see you as a foreman who was forced to do a difficult but necessary part of his job?

People hold grudges and spread the word when they feel they have been wronged. Don't allow it to happen to you.

BURNING BRIDGES

It's never a good idea to burn your bridges, but in our industry it's an especially bad way to go. Many people behave in a way that says, "I don't care if I've treated you inappropriately or insulted you. It just doesn't matter to me." Unfortunately, with this attitude there will surely come a time in your career when you'll be faced with a rude awakening precisely because there is no way for you to know who will end up on your project in the future.

Don't get so full of yourself that you start to believe your position as a foreman is etched in stone. The foremen I've known who have chosen to disregard the human aspect of the job have lived to regret it. I know because I've had a few of them walk onto my job site. When they see me they get the same haunted look in their eyes, the one that says, "I sure hope this guy doesn't remember how badly I treated him 'cause if he does I'm going to be in for a rough time."

Do you think I'd forget?

Finally, when you start to thin out your crew you will be under the scrutiny of the workers who remain behind. They want to see how you handle it. If they watch you give little or no notice at all, their respect for you will go down a notch. The people you are letting go are their coworkers, perhaps even their friends. They have been teammates in building the project day in and day out. They have spent many months working together for a common goal. The crew that stays behind to finish the project want to see that their teammates who are let go are let go with dignity and respect.

Do you want your remaining crew to lose respect for you? Do you want them to lose interest in helping you succeed? These are the questions to ask yourself because they will guide you in handling these difficult situations.

LOYALTY VS. FAVORITISM

In the construction industry, loyalty is a word tossed around to refer to a number of situations, but most of them smack more of favoritism than they do of integrity and trust between two or more people who work together. In my experience, these two words are misused frequently, both intentionally and unintentionally. When the use is intentional I have found it's because the person speaking has some hidden agenda or an axe to grind.

In essence, loyalty is the act of showing devotion, trustworthiness, and allegiance to another. Loyalty is something that is earned by virtue of an individual's consistent and positive actions.

Favoritism, on the other hand, is the act of showing bias, prejudice, or preferential treatment. Favoritism is often shown to an individual based on his relationship to the foreman rather than on his own merits. Favoritism is also utilized when a foreman attempts to gain favor with his direct supervisor or another company official. Sometimes this means protecting the relative of a supervisor who would otherwise be let go based on poor performance.

One of the highest accolades a foreman can receive from his peers is to be recognized as loyal to his employees, coworkers, and company.

Loyalty is a character trait that speaks volumes about who he is as an individual and a leader, and the label of loyalty carries with it many advantages as he moves from project to project throughout his career.

For example, when a reputation of loyalty precedes you on the job, any new working relationships you form (with new employees, foremen from other trades, or company management) will have the advantage of starting out on a solid foundation. Assured that you are trustworthy and held in high regard, these people will enter into a relationship with you willingly and with confidence that their expectations will be met.

Also, when people are convinced you are a respected and trusted leader, they will make a great effort to become a part of your winning team. This sets you up for building teams comprised of the best of the best in the field.

Finally, when it comes to your company, your loyalty towards them is just as important as their loyalty towards you. It is impossible for any contractor to run a successful company without skilled, dedicated, loyal foremen. As consumed as they are with keeping the business running, they have no choice but to rely on the integrity and unwavering determination of every foreman they employ.

How do you go about building a reputation of loyalty? It's really quite simple. You start by treating people the way you would expect to be treated if you were an integral crewmember on a successful project.

On-the-Job Training: Loyalty

You are the foreman running a long project. You have several individuals on your crew who are always going above and beyond what is asked of them. What do you do that will indicate to them that you are a foreman who cares about loyalty—both from and for your crew?

Easy question, right? First, make sure you keep these crewmembers until the very end of the project. Second, always communicate your appreciation to them and thank them for their contribution. Third, follow this conversation by informing them that you will do your best to hire them on another project at the conclusion of yours.

In order to make good on your word, talk to your supervisor about the important role these individuals have played in the success of your project. Do this far in advance of the time when your project will be completed, so the supervisor can begin the process of finding another project for these individuals. Call around to other foremen within your company and let them know you have some very talented people who will be looking for a new place to call home. Taking a few minutes to do these few steps and loyalty will be the word in people's minds when they hear your name.

All it really takes to build this kind of valuable reputation is consistently showing appreciation to those who help you do your job well. It's a win-win situation. Every time you show your loyalty to an individual, he becomes more loyal to you, and since you can't be the foreman and make all the installations on your own it's imperative that you have people working with you who are continually striving to exceed expectations.

MAINTAINING CREW MORALE

Now that you know what to do to run an efficient and productive job, take the information and apply it to produce a motivated crew and high morale. There's only one catch. When your job is running smoothly it starts to feel as if you can relax a little. But the reality is that this is no time to sit on your hands and wait for your project to become a success on its own.

I suggest spending a few minutes a week with your entire crew to discuss any difficulties they're having in the field. Welcome their concerns and opinions for finding solutions within the group; this will help you determine your course of action on an ongoing basis.

Motivating your crew has to be a continuous effort throughout the project. Morale on any project naturally ebbs and flows during its entire duration, but it's up to you to monitor your crew's pulse and make adjustments as necessary.

Leave your ego at home.

Overinflated and fragile egos have been the demise of many brilliant leaders throughout history. This is as true and prevalent in the construction industry as it is for every other business you can name. Take a minute to consider how an otherwise talented foreman's ego can sabotage his well-devised plans and derail his path to success. All you have to do is open a newspaper to read the headlines about

CEOs and presidents of corporations who are embroiled in scandals because their egos, coupled with their passionate desire for success and power, got the better of them. These are brilliant men and women whose lapses in judgment ultimately brought them only one thing: colossal failure.

Having a big ego is not in and of itself the problem. The controlling approach and intimidating demeanor is. Most people steer clear of the biggest ego in the room because they don't like the idea that they could get caught in the crossfire. This is true in corporate America and it is true on the construction site.

A foreman with a big ego is generally perceived as inapproachable by his crewmembers. His crew is uncomfortable bringing up questions and concerns. They would rather stick to themselves and gripe than go to him to voice the information he needs to hear.

Once you've lost your approachability to your crew, loss of morale is a short step away. These people are your first line of defense for identifying problems on the project. When they start keeping pertinent information to themselves, *look out.*

It's delusional to believe that if your crew isn't bringing you any problems it's because you're doing a wonderful job. If your crew seems too quiet, it's time for you to open up the dialogue and start asking the right questions so you can diagnose the issues. A foreman who reads his crew's silence as a sign that everything is great is a foreman who is choosing to avoid a burden that the truth might bring.

On the other hand, if you remain approachable and open to suggestions, you are guaranteed to save yourself unlimited amounts of time, energy, and grief. Don't be the self-absorbed foreman who believes that if his crew doesn't ask their questions the questions will go away, that a lack of desire on his crew's part is just something to put up with, or that production problems will eventually work themselves out.

None of these things is true. Ever.

With 20 years in the industry under my belt, here's the best advice I can give you:

Remain grounded. Respect your employees. Realize you can be replaced. Be the kind of leader you would like to work for yourself.

Everyone starts out a career with the best of intentions. But over time it can be difficult to keep from falling into the habit of taking yourself too seriously. If that happens you need to take a good hard look at the reasons behind your attitude, or before you know it you'll be driven by your ego and perceived as arrogant.

Here's one suggestion for keeping yourself humble.

Any time you feel your ego is controlling your decision making and how you are treating the people around you...STOP. Remind yourself of one thing, just two little words: NOBODY CARES. That's right. These two words will bring you back down to earth faster than the proverbial apple can fall from the tree.

Why? Because what matters to people when they come to work is that they feel productive and appreciated, and that they have a sense of job security. That's it. The whole *enchilada*. A foreman who spends more time praising himself than praising his crew cannot make this happen.

Do your job. Do it well. This is all you need to know. Respect and adulation will follow.

FINAL THOUGHTS

I'm sure by this point you are fully aware of the common theme running throughout this book: that your success as a foreman is directly tied to your crew's success, and that your crew's success is based on their having everything they need from nuts and bolts to appreciation and motivation.

Being a foreman is not about you and what makes your life easier and more comfortable; it is about setting your crew up to meet or exceed the goals that you set out for them.

Your crew's needs are far more important to fulfil than your own. Even when you are feeling the heavy pressure and anxiety that inevitably comes with running a large project, be convincingly confident and determined to your crew. Their perception of your conviction and ability is what shapes their attitudes and morale.

Your crew looks to you for direction and assurance. If you remain positive and upbeat even when things aren't going the way you planned, your crew will likely go along for the ride.

Chapter 24

Difficult Employees and Other Trades

To this point we've been discussing strategies that can be utilized to ensure you have a crew that will be behind you and your plan and that is committed to achieving your production goals. Unfortunately, no matter how hard you try and no matter how well you treat people, there will always be a small percentage of individuals dedicated to causing trouble.

DIFFICULT EMPLOYEES

Nothing is more frustrating than having a good crew, a good plan, and all the tools and material to complete every task only to have an employee who, for some unknown reason, chooses to be difficult. It only takes one person stirring up trouble and controversy to send your whole project into a tailspin. That's why how you handle an individual like this is very important.

Troublemakers need to be dealt with swiftly and directly. If you hesitate, look the other way because you are uncomfortable confronting them, or choose to believe the problem will go away on its own, your inaction will have a lasting negative affect on your crew and on your project.

It is your responsibility as the foreman to acknowledge when you have a problem, take the necessary steps to isolate that problem, and then implement a viable solution. We already talked about how to have a conversation with someone who is causing trouble and about how it may be necessary to terminate him if this conversation fails. Either way something must be done to keep your project on track.

Here is the tiered approach I have found to be the most successful:

I always start with a one-on-one conversation, *away from the rest of the crew*. If you make the mistake of trying to change this individual's behavior by calling negative attention to him in front of your crew you will only force him to become more defensive. I have seen this tactic attempted numerous times and always with the same results: the foreman ends up looking like the bad guy.

A crew frequently takes the "us against them" attitude when it comes to the relationship between them and "management." Which, by the way, now includes you. If that happens, instead of having a problem with one person you could find yourself in the position of having the additional task of trying to regain the trust and respect of the other crewmembers.

During my private conversation with this individual, I take the professional approach. I offer him an opportunity to work on changing his behavior patterns. I talk to him about the way I see things and give him an opportunity to explain the way he sees it. If you actually listen to his response, you might be surprised to hear he has some valid points about why he is having such a hard time fitting into your system.

If you enter the conversation with an open mind you'll improve your chances of success exponentially. If your mind set is more of the "If this guy gets out of line with me, if he says one thing I don't agree with, I'm going to can him on the spot" mentality, you'll get nowhere.

Don't start out by being aggressive and making threats. Not only is behavior like that unprofessional, but very counterproductive to what you are trying to accomplish. A less than professional approach undermines your reputation as it relates to managing all difficult situations. Take a tough but fair standpoint, and make it very clear to the individual that you believe there is an issue that requires immediate resolution.

THE INTENTIONAL DISRUPTOR

Sometimes during your conversation you'll learn the unfortunate truth that this individual is being intentionally difficult or disruptive. If this is the case, then recognize that you have put this person in a very uncomfortable position. Interestingly, this can work in your favor. Since most foremen don't have the nerve or the people skills to handle a situation as you are now doing, an employee like this may be caught off guard by your approach. As a strategy it can therefore be very effective.

Because most people expect to hear, "If you don't like the way I do things then there's the door," when you confront the problem head on and allow them the respectful opportunity to explain their way of thinking, you virtually remove any excuse they have ready for behaving in the same manner in the future.

With this approach you create the opportunity for things to turn around quickly.

Although during your conversation the individual will likely not share many details, and in fact will generally insist that everything is fine (that he is just having a bad day, week, or month), from the time of your conversation forward his behavior will improve. This happens for three reasons: (1) he now knows you are not afraid to confront him; (2) he knows his actions are being monitored; and (3) he knows if he really needs to get something off his chest, he has been given the opportunity.

Furthermore, since you have also established a day and time that the matter has been discussed, the employee has been put on notice and a verbal warning has been issued. He knows you have it documented and that you intend to keep the documentation in case you need it in the future.

Whenever conversations like this occur, documentation is always a fact of life. Document everything you can about the interaction, such as the day, time, topics discussed, conclusions reached, and everyone's responsibility moving forward. Inform your supervisor about the situation, what you are doing to attempt to resolve the issue, and document that you have done so. Not only might your supervisor offer some suggestions, but you don't want any surprises if you are put in the position of having to terminate the employee down the road.

If after having the conversation the employee continues to be difficult and to cause problems on your project, approach him one more time. Give him a last chance to change direction. I can hear the groans now. "Why should I give him another chance when I've already talked to him about it?"

I agree that this individual should have gotten the hint already, but in the interest of trying to be understanding and fair, I always try to give people the chance to turn it around, to see that I am giving them every benefit of the doubt. With most people, in most cases, this will earn you trust and respect.

However, this is also the point where the conversation needs to change direction as well. This conversation differs from the first in that now you must give the individual a direct warning that his job is on the line. You must be very clear about what is at stake. The conversation also needs to conclude with your letting him know that although the decision is his, not yours, in terms of changing his behavior, you will not hesitate to act accordingly based on his actions. Let him know there will be no more warnings.

As is to be expected, even with the best of intentions to work things out civilly and productively, the results you want will not necessarily be the results you get. It comes with the territory that when you are a foreman there are times when you'll run out of options and have to terminate a disgruntled employee in the best interest of your project. Your instinct about when it is the best time to cut your losses comes with time and experience.

DIFFICULTY WITH OTHER TRADES

Handling a difficult trade is similar to handling any difficult employee or situation, minus the critical element of your ability to fire the trade. A productive solution, however, is still based on good communication and an attempt to get to the bottom of why the problem exists. Many of the strategies you'll use to deal with difficult foremen from other trades will come from your growing experience. Here are a few suggestions that can help.

First, if you're having trouble working with another foreman from another trade, don't wait. Start a conversation the same way you would with an employee: one on one in an area away from other people. Don't do it in a meeting! Don't do it in front of other people to prove one-upsmanship! If you do, you'll get no cooperation at all.

Keep in mind that most people see what they're doing as part of their job in protecting the interests of their company, which is exactly what *you're* doing. They may not see their actions as being difficult. Not only that, they may think *you're* the one being difficult. Again, I remind you to enter the conversation with an open mind and the willingness to listen to the other foreman's perspective.

Let the foreman know that your primary goal is to find some common ground to build a working relationship that is beneficial to you both. Don't be accusatory and one-sided. State your issue along with how it is affecting your progress, and describe what you would like to see done differently. Hopefully the person will be reasonable and try to accommodate your requests.

Before concluding the conversation, make it clear to this individual that he is welcome to come to you if he needs help working out any issues he might have. It bears repeating that when you speak to people in a rational, productive, and respectful way positive results are much more likely to occur.

Following your discussion, in which you hopefully reached some solutions, don't expect that things will change overnight. It generally takes just as long to unlearn old habits as it does to create new ones. It may take a reminder here and there to prompt this individual's memory of the agreement you made earlier, but be as patient as you can if he seems to be making a good faith effort.

If after a fair amount of time, however, you still can't seem to get him to cooperate, it may be time to seek out help. Talk to the general contractor first. Since subcontractors generally work directly for the general contractor, he will hold some authority to step in if he sees the need for it. If this action doesn't seem to move things forward in a positive direction, you may have to ask your supervisor to contact the other foreman's supervisor to see if they can't work something out. The obvious problem with this approach is that any foreman who is reprimanded or even spoken to by his supervisor about how he's doing his job is going to come away with a little bit of hostility towards whoever brought it up.

In closing, I'd like to state that over the years I have rarely met another foreman who was so difficult to work with that we couldn't find some way to work together. Sometimes it takes a little creativity and a lot of open communication, but you can usually get where you want to go.

Chapter 25

Be a Leader

In this final chapter on people skills I want to restate what I believe to be one of the most important aspects of being a foreman: that your first and last responsibility every day is to be the best leader you can be.

Your company has proven their faith in your skills as a trades person and as a leader by assigning you to a foreman position. Give them every reason to believe they have made the right decision.

When times get tough, remember that they are counting on you to protect their interests and to do everything in your power to make the project a success. At times it will be a heavy burden to carry, but you have to stay steadfast in your commitment and push through any adversity.

Remember to lead your crew to success. Provide them with everything they need to do their jobs and keep them engaged by communicating their value to you and the project. Your crew looks to you for guidance and needs to understand your vision, and there is no one else who can provide these things to them. Give them the confidence to believe that when you succeed they will succeed as well. A crew who believes in their leader will work hard and exceed expectations. As they witness the effort and energy you bring to the project combined with your dedication to quality, efficiency, and production, they will feel empowered to mimic your actions.

The construction industry is overrun with mediocre, run of the mill foremen who do just enough to get by. The kind of leader you choose to be and the seriousness and dedication with which you take your responsibilities defines who you are and how far you will go.

There are many rungs on the ladder of success and prosperity. Along those steps you are certain to come across obstacles that get in the way of your climb to the top. Your level of success will be determined by how you deal with any setbacks that leave you stalled along the way.

It takes sheer determination and intestinal fortitude to stay on the path to attaining the ultimate career goals you set for yourself. Anyone can learn what it takes to be a great foreman, but not everyone can apply those theories in the real world. My advice? Stay focused, be committed, and have confidence in your abilities.

Using the people skills you have learned in this section, you can now approach and manage difficult situations with the confidence that comes from knowing you are capable of finding solutions that produce acceptable outcomes for all parties involved. Since learning to communicate effectively and to motivate others is a never-ending process, you should never stop searching for new and innovative techniques. If you keep your mind open to new ideas and respect the people you work with, success will surely follow.

STRESS MANAGEMENT

Chapter 26

Stress Awareness

Stress is serious business. Because the construction industry by nature is a very stressful environment, for those of us who find ourselves in a foreman position this stress gets ratcheted up tenfold. If you let them, factors like tight schedules or running a project that was bid incorrectly will have the power to drain you mentally and generate trouble for you in every aspect of your life. You may find yourself having trouble sleeping, experiencing strained personal relationships, with a dependency on drugs or alcohol, or coping with stress-related illnesses that cause your health to deteriorate to dangerous levels.

I have personally watched stress negatively impact too many good people to ignore its existence and not spend the time to talk about it here.

Taking stress as seriously as you take every other part of your job is the first step toward controlling the effect it has on you. Heavy doses of stress will stay with you 24 hours a day, which is why it is so vital that you maintain a healthy perspective about what is most important. Your job is important, your career is important, and commitments made to your company and customers are important, but if you don't have your health or family none of these things will matter.

IS STRESS PREVENTABLE?

Stress is unavoidable. It's a fact of life. It is a consequence of your chosen profession. But it is also manageable. Learning to cope with the many pressures that come with running work is an absolute must if you want to avoid having it infiltrate the other facets of your life. Throughout your career you will need to continually monitor your stress levels and take measures to prevent it from consuming you. If your goal is to have a long, productive, and rewarding career, then managing stress is not optional.

One of the first things to appreciate is that there are some stress factors that are preventable and some that are not. This first consideration is important because you have enough other things to worry about without wasting valuable time and energy trying to fix what you can't control. Plus, there is an added level of frustration that comes with believing you can change something that in reality you cannot.

In order to get the maximum value from this chapter, I ask that you be honest with yourself when contemplating your shortcomings. Only then can you begin to focus on adopting new habits and making strides toward relieving some of the pressures you face.

STRESS AND UNPREPAREDNESS

You know what stresses me out? The thought of my crew standing around and not working because I haven't provided them with what they need. For each person standing there I imagine a dollar sign over his head next to numbers that are rolling backwards. The numbers start to spin faster and faster the more time it takes me to get them back to being productive.

One of the reasons this conscious nightmare causes me so much anxiety is because first, I know it is preventable and second, I know it is my responsibility to keep it from happening. Whenever this occurs on one of my projects there is only one conclusion to be reached: that I haven't planned well enough to prevent it.

Lack of preparedness is one of the most common and preventable forms of stress a foreman encounters. When you are faced with the challenge of a question you should be able to answer or a tool that should have been on site already but isn't, it's easy to give the impression that you are irritated or angry with the person doing the asking. It's not uncommon for those in leadership roles to have an aversion to admitting they're unprepared or unwilling to take full responsibility when a mistake has been made. Construction foremen are no exception.

On-the-Job Training: What's Up?

You have been feeling rushed and uneasy for days. You find yourself mad at your crewmembers when they ask you questions. What's going on?

That uneasy and frustrated feeling you have when you are caught unprepared is called stress or anxiety. If you stop for a second and think about what the root causes of these feelings are, you will see that whatever situation is facing you might have been avoided by better preparation.

Are you mad at one of your crewmembers for asking a question? You shouldn't be. You need people like him who, when they are unclear about the details of a task, come to you and ask.

Are you embarrassed that you don't have the answer right on the tip of your tongue? You shouldn't be. This is your ego running the show between your ears! There is no possible way you can feasibly have the answer to all questions that arise.

Do you think your crewmembers should simply do their job without the tools they need instead of bothering you? I sure hope not, but this is the vibe you give off when you know the reason for their constant requests is that you have been neglectful and have shirked your responsibility.

No foreman wants to be considered unprepared or out of control by his crew. The good news is that all the things that might cause your crew to feel this way about you are actually within in your power to control. If you let all the things you have to do and the project deadlines looming over your head cause you to become irritable, defensive, and short-tempered, your crew will respond in kind.

On-the-Job-Training: Stressed?

> You've been feeling rushed and stressed all week. You show up to your meeting unprepared, figuring you'll just wing it. When you get there you feel both uncomfortable about the meeting and antsy to return to the project, where you know you're behind schedule.

When you show up to a meeting, such as a coordination meeting, without having first putting some effort into designing a decisive plan that spells out how you intend to execute your part of an upcoming phase of the project, you will feel the heat. If you haven't taken the time to study the drawings of the other trades and don't have at least a basic understanding about their installation, you will come across as uninformed. Given Murphy's law, you can also be sure that precisely because you are unprepared you will be asked about the specifics regarding your installation.

When you show up and try to shoot from the hip it becomes very obvious to everyone in the meeting that you are not fully aware of the larger scope of the project. This is not only unfair to the other trades involved, but unfair to your company. For every detail you miss due to a lack of interest, desire, or commitment, you put another trade at risk of working inefficiently or having to do extra work due to your complacency. Your company suffers consequences as well in the form of wasted labor hours incurred by mistakes and re-work, which add up to a loss in profitability.

The net result? Considerable hostility directed at you that will ultimately manifest itself in the form of more stress, both mental and physical.

PREVENTION

Again, even though we can't prevent stress altogether, there are many methods for setting it aside and working it through. They take a little more time and effort, but are always worth the investment. This final suggestion is my solution for making it less likely you will ever find your crew standing around because they've caught you off guard.

On the very first day a new crewmember arrives on your job site I encourage you to give him a full explanation of how you run your project and what you expect. He will have worked with a variety of personalities over his career, as all your crewmembers will have, so it always helps to explain your way of doing things. It might be as simple as telling him you expect him to keep his work area well organized and cleaned up at all times or that your biggest pet peeve is employees who are late.

One of the best strategies you can implement to lower your stress is to request that your crewmembers inform you in advance when they expect to finish a task.

When a crewmember gives you advance notice that a task is about to be completed, he is providing you with the time to properly assess what direction you want him to take next. There is a big difference between specifically asking someone to do this for you and assuming he is going to do it, however. Most people have no problem keeping you informed of their progress, but what you may not realize is that people who have never been in your position don't understand how finding something out at the last minute can, at least temporarily, affect the flow of an entire project.

THE DIFFICULT EMPLOYEE RETURNS

Yes, I know we talked about problem employees in the last part of this book. But we need to bring it up here again because in my experience there will always be those individuals who somehow manage to wait until they are finished with a project before telling you they need a new one. Is this intentional? It doesn't really matter. Because either way there is a solution to the problem.

First, ask the individual to cooperate. Doesn't work? Then pull out your ace in the hole.

There are always jobs that people on your crew don't want to do if they have the choice. You are undoubtedly fully aware of what these jobs are—anything from digging a ditch or running a jackhammer. For the employee who refuses to think ahead, simply save one of these tasks for him. I might say, "Gee, I wish I'd known you were almost finished. I would have found something else for you to do. But since I didn't know, right now all I have is this ditch to dig."

After a couple of undesirable tasks are sent his way, it only makes sense that the employee will decide it's in his best interest to cooperate...and to learn to help you be more prepared.

UNPREDICTABLE STRESS

Many things about the construction industry are unpredictable. Deliveries that don't arrive when expected, issues due to weather, or another trade's inability to pass an inspection. Countless variables are out of your control. That's why my advice is to control what you can and have a contingency plan for when the unexpected happens. Knowing you have a backup plan, whether you end up needing it or not, should help to drop your blood pressure. Contingency plans aren't meant to be used as your only plans; they are there as your safety net should you need one.

In Part II on planning I stressed the importance of detailed advanced planning for increasing efficiency and production. I now suggest that there is another benefit of having a long list of tasks that your employees can accomplish while you deal with any unanticipated circumstance that puts a crimp in your direction. This thorough plan you have at your disposal is your ticket to sanity when you are thrown a curve ball.

I don't know how many times I've walked into work with a very specific list of tasks and goals I wanted to complete that day only to have something change my direction and steer me totally off course. At the end of the day I'm left thinking, *Shoot, I didn't get one thing done that I wanted to accomplish today.* It used to drive me totally crazy. All through the day I'd focus on trying to get back on track, getting more and more frustrated by all the things and people who were keeping from accomplishing what I had set out to do.

I finally had to accept that in our business no plan is etched in stone, and that we must be cooperative and flexible in order for every trade on the project to succeed.

There will be days when people come at you from all directions, all needing something NOW. Remember, don't kill the messenger. It's not your crewmember's fault you are having a busy or bad day, week, or month. Every person who approaches you more than likely has a legitimate question or concern, and each of them believes what he needs is extremely important.

Here is what I do when I feel this kind of day starting to unfold. As soon as I get the feeling things are spiraling out of control or that I can't seem to get a firm grasp on everything being asked of me, I stop, consider what is most important, and then set out to methodically work through every issue by writing each item down and putting it in order of importance.

Doing this only takes a few minutes and having a written list helps me maintain my focus. Plus, it leaves me no chance of forgetting something. Every time an issue is solved I check it off and move on to the next. This feels good!

Don't let your mind wander to items that are further down the list when you are working on items toward the top; this will only cloud and clutter your thoughts until you find yourself in the same predicament as before, out of control and unable to focus. Remember, you can only do one thing at a time if you expect to do it well.

Unpredictable stress can also cause us to make excuses and lay blame, but this only undermines any respect or credibility you have built with your crew. A good foreman doesn't point fingers when things don't go as planned; he takes responsibility and finds solutions.

To help you diagnose and then eliminate factors that cause you the most stress ask the following questions:

Are they coming from a lack of planning on your part or are they solely due to unforeseen circumstances?

Is it possible that your ego is playing a role?

Are you unwilling to say the words, "I don't know, let me do some research, I'll get back to you with an answer as soon as I can," to a question from an employee?

If the answer to any of these questions is yes then you are definitely putting unrealistic pressure on yourself. Not only that, every time you give someone an answer that may not be correct, you are creating opportunities for mistakes to be made. Take ownership of the things you can control and do your best to handle the rest in a way that keeps the project flowing and doesn't send you into a tailspin.

IDENTIFYING STRESS

Sometimes the best thing you can do is to attempt to identify what your particular stress factors are. One way is to step back, analyze your typical day, and then pinpoint where and when you feel the most stress.

On-the-Job Training: Coordination

You have found that every time you have a coordination meeting with the various foremen from the other trades on your project you get stressed out. For the whole day leading up to these meetings you find yourself agitated and on edge. Even if you walk into the meeting feeling okay, by the time you leave you have a pit in your stomach like a basketball. What can you do?

My suggestion is to play these meetings over in your mind and make an effort to identify at which point you usually begin feeling uncomfortable. It might be that every time you are in a meeting you become a favorite target of the general contractor because your crew is not picking up after themselves. Maybe, as mentioned before, you repeatedly show up unprepared or are frequently having trouble making your schedules. Repetitive behaviors like these will cause you to lose the respect of the other foremen on the project.

Take the first step by identifying and acknowledging which of your stress factors have been exacerbated at your own hand due to a lack of focus or a failure to prioritize your daily responsibilities. One simple solution is to communicate with your crew that you need their cooperation in order to stay off the hot seat when you go to your meetings. If your crew likes and respects you, the last thing they want is to be a contributing factor for your getting reprimanded by the project superintendant. In this case, one simple conversation with your crew can totally eliminate one of your stress factors.

When it comes to things that take more time and focus like studying prints and preparing plans to stay within the project's time line, there is only one thing to do. You must find a time when you are the least likely to be interrupted and get it done. This is your responsibility. No one else can do it for you.

Is scheduling causing you stress? If so, ask yourself the following questions:

Are you giving your crew the opportunity to be as efficient and productive as possible?

Are you being realistic about the capability of your current number of crewmembers to complete every task that is on the present schedule?

If the answers are yes to both of these questions then I suggest asking your crew if there is anything you can do for them to boost their existing level of production. Some foremen find this challenging because they think they should be able to come up with all the answers. Don't overlook one of your greatest resources: the minds of your crewmembers. These are the people who see the project from a different perspective and can provide possible options.

If a conversation with your crew doesn't produce any feasible solutions, then I suggest talking to your project manager about the challenges you're facing. Remember, the further behind you get the more overwhelmed you become and the less likely your chances will be for turning in a successful and profitable project.

Most problems and stress factors have reasonable solutions. Sometimes these solutions take a while to find and sometimes they come from unlikely places. The key is to avoid the mind set of believing there are some problems that can't be fixed because this mind set only allows you to surrender to the stress that accompanies those problems. With that kind of defeatist attitude you will be destined for a long career of anxiety, stress, and pressure.

FINAL THOUGHTS

Since I am very clear on the fact that I do not know what every foreman is thinking I don't want to come as if I do. But I have worked for enough foremen over the years to form some general opinions about how communication, or lack thereof, between a foreman and his crew affects the outcome of a project as well as the foreman's ultimate stress level.

Many foremen rarely (sometimes never!) address their crew as a whole. After witnessing the negative effects of this strategy on multiple projects, I made it a personal goal to figure out why so many foremen suffered from poor communication skills, including the decision to avoid communicating with their crew.

I asked myself why a foreman would choose to keep his crew in the dark about upcoming phases and associated schedules...why he would feel uncomfortable speaking in front of a group or fear the possibility of not knowing the answers to every question asked of him.

The only answer I have come up with is that most of these foremen have never received any training on the subject of communication. They have no idea that there are better strategies out there for handling their stress-related problems. Therefore, they come to the conclusion that the only thing to do is to put up a good front, a façade to make everyone believe that they are in control, have all the answers, never make mistakes, and don't feel the effects of stress.

What is the result? Only more stress...and a long career burdened by loneliness and isolation. The bigger you build yourself up to be, the harder you'll fall when the day comes that you can't live up to your own hype.

Exhibiting genuine humility is the best way to lower stress and is always the sign of a great leader.

When all is said and done, becoming a successful foreman is only worth it to you and your family if you are happy and have your health. If you deal with stress by abusing drugs or alcohol, have a nervous break down, or drop dead, you *will* be replaced. I am not saying your company doesn't care about you or that it will sweep you to the side if you face some adversity. I am merely stating an obvious outcome of these scenarios. It is a harsh reality, but the business and the project you are running will go on without you if you make a sudden exit.

That's why longevity in this business comes down to balancing your work life and your personal life. You are perfectly capable of taking your work responsibilities seriously without taking yourself too seriously.

Chapter 27

Self-preservation

Let's continue with the idea of self-preservation. Included under the tactical umbrella of self-preservation is taking all the steps you can take to safeguard your physical, mental, and emotional well-being as you navigate through your career—in other words, to keep stress from controlling your life. This includes making good, timely decisions regarding what you are willing to do as well as what you are not willing to do. It also encompasses your integrity, your willingness to stand up for yourself, and your ability to make tough decisions that may put your ambitions of moving up the ladder in the slow lane.

As I've said many times before, the construction industry is filled with stress and pressure-filled days, weeks, months, and years. Some of the decisions you make as a foreman will be small and seemingly inconsequential, but there are going to be times in your career where a decision you make could affect your employability, future opportunities, and what level of success you reach.

There is no way to discuss this topic without making it sound weighty because in many ways it is. What I hope is that reading this book gives you the confidence to know that you make your own luck in this business, and that you shouldn't let people take advantage of you just because they're offering you an opportunity you don't think you can find somewhere else.

Here is what I know. When you have exceptional trade and leadership skills, opportunities find *you*. It is not necessary to take on foreman positions that are obviously set up for you to fail. I am not insinuating that you should be concerned someone is out to get you. I am merely suggesting that you avoid agreeing to run a project that is clearly doomed from the start without first discussing on whose shoulders the responsibility will fall should the project lose more money than the company anticipates.

On-the-Job Training: Incorrect Bid

You have been asked to run a project for a company you have worked for before. This time you find out that the company has been awarded the project, but has bid it incorrectly. But at this point it will be either very difficult or impossible for the contractor to get out of building the project, especially if he wants to maintain a good reputation and credibility with the customer, and, even more importantly, with the industry. Bailing out on the contract would surely play a role in whether the customer would ever invite the contractor to bid on any future projects.

What do you do? My recommendation is this: Every time you are asked to be the foreman on any project, large or small, ask questions. Don't let ego, pride, desperation, or disillusionment steer you into making a poor decision that could leave a long-lasting dark shadow over your career.

There will be times when a project manager and/or company's estimation team isn't completely forthcoming about information, as described above on this underbid project. Naturally no one wants to be held responsible for the results. This less than full disclosure doesn't stop with the owner either, who still has to find a foreman willing to run the project.

As much as I wish I could tell you that this type of thing doesn't happen, it does. This is why I am stressing that you take care of yourself and manage your career decisions wisely. Don't be the person who blindly takes on a project to appease someone else. The worst part is that at the conclusion of projects like these, ones that are destined to lose money from the very beginning, when it is time to answer for the poor results the foreman is often the one left holding the bag.

If you ever get the feeling that an opportunity will be taken away from you because you are asking too many questions or you are expressing concern that something isn't quite right with a project, put on the brakes right there. You'll be able to walk away satisfied, knowing that you avoided what could have been a career-damaging situation.

In the meantime, because it is more than likely that at some point in your career a company for which you're working will be awarded a project that has been underbid, I want to offer you some tools to handle this difficult situation.

In the spirit of being a team player, I don't believe you should instantly turn down the prospect of running a project just on the basis of its being underbid. What I certainly recommend you do is discuss the entire project, at length, with your management team, including what the best and worse case scenarios might be at the project's completion. Is breaking even an acceptable outcome? What if the project comes in at 3% over the pre-job expected outcome? Will repercussions be levied against the person who accepts the role of foreman if the job goes completely upside down?

Make sure all of these questions are answered to your satisfaction before you ever consider taking the lead on a losing job. If they aren't, then it is my opinion you'd be better off declining the position.

On the other hand, *if* you and your company can agree the project has issues and is likely to lose money, and *if* you and your company acknowledge that you are being put in the foreman position to mitigate the potential loss, accepting the position can still have a positive outcome for your career and your relationship with that company.

Finally, don't forget to document every pre-job conversation and meeting that takes place and the conclusions that were reached prior to taking this job. Again, it has been my experience that when a project goes sideways and people are scrambling to protect their hides they can suddenly fall under some kind of amnesic spell.

It has to be said that not everyone plays above board and not everyone is willing to back up what he says or does. I would like to tell you that I trusted every project manager with whom I have ever worked in my career, but I can't. Years of experience and witnessing people at their worst has taught me to question people's true intentions.

However, just as I've done, you will build many long-term and productive working relationships with good people. These are the individuals with whom you want to align yourself, not the ones who will sell you out at a moment's notice to benefit their own careers.

BE YOUR OWN COMPANY

In the same way your company spends time, money, and energy protecting its interests in the marketplace, you need to spend time and energy protecting your name and reputation. After all, once you become a foreman, your current company and potential future employers will base their decision on whether to put you in charge of a project on your reputation for providing successful and profitable results.

REASONABLE EXPECTATIONS

As the foreman of any project, you are entitled to your own list of reasonable expectations—things that you believe you need to do the best job you can. By the same token, your company's management team is responsible for holding a pre-job meeting to communicate what is expected of you as a foreman.

Remember, "pre-job" means exactly that: *before* the beginning of the project. If the company doesn't utilize a pre-job meeting format, then I suggest you request such a meeting before you agree to take on the project. As I've said before, every construction project is unique and no two buildings are alike. Therefore, the people who are responsible for bidding your project likely hold preconceived notions about the direction you should take when putting your plan together.

We talked earlier about the fact that typically the estimator and project manager make determinations about the building process during the bidding phase, and how this information is extremely valuable to any foreman setting out to devise a comprehensive plan. Details about the materials to be used, vendors chosen to supply the materials, and installation methods are way too important to be brushed aside.

Even though you may have run many projects in your career, it might be that the one you are about to begin will be more difficult than anything you have ever built. A health care facility is not the same as an industrial plant, and an industrial plant is not the same as a high-tech manufacturing facility.

I find the pre-job meeting to be one of the most crucial aspects of any project in terms of the future dynamics and relationships of the team throughout the length of the job. This is your chance to ask questions, document conclusions, and make sure all of the bases are covered. You can't just sit quietly and assume that everyone will give you all the information you need.

Don't let your fear of losing an opportunity be the reason that you don't ask tough questions. If you are in a pre-job meeting and no one else brings up a subject that you find important, I encourage you to do so. I'll bet at least one other person in the room will appreciate that you did.

HONESTY IS THE BEST POLICY

You can be sure that at the conclusion of your project, especially if it has lost money, you will be called into a meeting to discuss how and why your project failed to make a profit. I can promise you that the same individuals on your management team who chose to ignore the importance of making a pre-job meeting a priority will be there with a list of questions for you.

My suggestion is that you bring all of your documentation about pre-job conversations and any other pertinent information that will demonstrate that you did the best you could with what you had to work with. Don't make excuses. If there are things you could have done better, own up to them. Explain what you learned from the experience and how you plan to implement what you have learned to increase the probability of success on future projects.

People respect honesty. Admit your mistakes humbly and then move forward.

Pre-job meetings not only set expectations, but set the tone for any cooperative venture. Large construction projects require the cooperation of everyone involved, including office staff, crewmembers, foremen, and project managers. A pre-job meeting will outline everyone's responsibilities on that particular project, which will help to eliminate any misunderstandings that may lead to problems on site. A meeting of this sort should also be documented in the form of a written record that will serve to hold all individuals present accountable.

Sooner or later we all work with someone who tries to skate by and do the minimum while everyone around him carries the load. A meeting like this can motivate someone with a tendency to slack off to put forth a little more effort. It's the unfortunate part of any profession that we have to resort to safeguards to make sure people do their jobs, but when it is your reputation on the line, you do what you have to do.

EXPECTATIONS FROM ABOVE

As a foreman, you should always be given the opportunity to ask questions about the project. Even if it doesn't happen in the form of a sit-down meeting with the entire management team, in-depth conversations with anyone who has been or will be involved in the project will serve you well.

At the point at which you are asked to lead a project the estimators and project managers should be your primary sources of information. At this point they know more about the project than anyone else and there is valuable information to be gained by asking them the right questions. These people should be willing, able, and happy to pass on any information that may be pertinent for you.

Beware of the ones that won't.

In the past, I have experienced varying degrees of cooperation on the part of estimators and project managers. In most cases when there has been a lack of cooperation it has been because their time and focus was being consumed by projects currently in progress or by future projects still in the estimating phase. Are these valid reasons for ignoring your request for information? No.

This is why it is imperative that you always protect your own interests. *This is the nature of self-preservation.* Your success, sanity, and reputation are all riding on a team effort, and your company's management team is part of that cooperative unit.

TAKING YOUR TIME

Far too many foremen are in such a big hurry to reach their career goals that they make ill-advised decisions regarding projects that may be beyond their expertise at the time. Everyone wants a foreman who is ambitious and confident in his abilities, but once again I advise you to think things through and make timely decisions when it comes to your career. Being under-qualified to run certain projects shouldn't be a blow to your ego because everyone has strengths and weaknesses in different facets of his job.

It is my opinion that due to the nature of construction, we all have holes in our abilities at some level even after gaining years of experience. Determining factors include the contractors for whom you've worked, the people with whom you've worked, and the particular market where you live and work. Maybe you have considerable experience working on industrial plants, but haven't had the opportunity to work on high-tech manufacturing facilities. These two types of projects are worlds apart in how they need to be managed.

It is always your decision how far you want to push yourself outside your comfort zone, but if you are asked to run a project you believe is over your head, I suggest you explain these concerns to your contractor. Talking about your thoughts doesn't mean you won't end up running the project. What it will do is give you and your company a chance to talk about the areas where you believe you need some improvement. Your company may even suggest putting someone else in the foreman position and having the two of you work side by side so you can gain experience through watching how he operates.

The people who make the decisions about who should run each project are very busy and may not always consider whether or not you are ready to move up to the next level. Don't get so full of yourself that you think you are ready to tackle a difficult project when inside you know you aren't. Trust me, waiting until the end of a project, one that you rode into the ground, is no time to tell your management team you should have never been given it to begin with.

Advance your career and advancements at a pace that is acceptable to you, and don't let anyone force you into a position that may damage your reputation. You have your entire career to run the larger and higher profile projects, but only after you have established yourself as a well-rounded foreman.

On the flip side, there will always be those foremen who have so much pride or eagerness to move up the ladder that they are less than forthcoming about their abilities. You'll know who these people are when you're working with them on a project and they are obviously overwhelmed by the project's breadth and complexity. I'm the first to admit this can happen—as it did to me on my own first project, which I feel suffered immensely due to my lack of experience.

BE TRUE TO YOURSELF

It seems there's always one more trap to avoid, doesn't it?

This one involves getting into a competition with other foremen at your company; in other words, attempting to measure your career progress against theirs. This does not work! Instead, take things at your own pace, be honest with yourself about your abilities, and be up front with your company. This is the correct path to becoming a better foreman. Your intention should be to make good decisions that will prevent blemishes on your record that may negatively affect any future opportunities.

This shouldn't come as a surprise, but sometimes project managers intentionally play foremen against each other in order to push them to excel. See this behavior for what it is and don't play into it. If someone is "better" than you, so what? There will always be foremen who have more experience and skill. On the other hand, don't become complacent when it comes to learning new and valuable methods for doing your job.

Your main objective? Earn your respect as a foreman through your consistent long-term successes. Think about it this way, if you are labelled the "best" foreman around but only work eight months a year, will you still be satisfied?

FINAL THOUGHTS

This entire chapter has been dedicated to you and your long-term sanity, reputation, and success. None of these components holds more weight than the others, but if at the end of your career you can't honestly say you have achieved all three, I'm not sure you will feel completely fulfilled.

Do you think anyone else will remember that at year six of a 35-year career you turned down a job? Probably not. That's why you are the only one who can decide at what point in your career you are willing and able to tackle projects that stretch every aspect of your professional life.

Chapter 28

Asking For Help

If there's one thing I know about construction workers, it's that many of them refuse to ask for help no matter how much they need it.

No matter how difficult the task, these individuals believe that if they ask for help they are admitting they are weak or incompetent. I suspect this mentality is instilled in some of us from the very outset of our careers (or lives).

Unfortunately, the problem doesn't stop there. As long as I've been in construction, and I'd venture to say for many generations before, I've seen how people make a sport out of giving others a hard time, feeding into any feelings of inadequacy they may have. Even if teasing someone else is meant to be "in good fun," when it's added to the fear of appearing weak or incapable the negative impact on the individual's psyche can be felt throughout his working years.

I can still remember working as a material handler at the age of 16. The old timers teased me mercilessly day in and day out. As I struggled with a heavy piece of conduit I'd hear, "Come on, you gotta be tough if you're going to make it in this business." Sometimes they'd call out to one of their coworkers to come on over to enjoy the show. I knew and liked most of these people so it didn't bother me much at the time—at least not as badly as it might have under different circumstances. But looking back at those incidents 20 years later, it's easy for me to see that what appeared on the surface to be the good-natured ribbing of coworkers actually did some damage. Yes, I learned quickly to suck it up, to act as if the ribbing was just another part of the work, but now I know how this ended up working against me because sucking it up helped create some of the least productive habits and belief systems I still hold today. One of these is the unwillingness to ask for help.

It all comes down to pride. Too much pride is never a good thing. Yes, have pride in your work and your professionalism, but don't be so concerned about what people think of you that you pass up opportunities to gain valuable information from those with more experience.

This is an example of a conversation I have probably had with myself a hundred times in my career. It starts out like this: *I'm not to sure how to handle this challenge, but I know if I called Bob up he could get me going in the right direction.*

Then I think, *But if I call Bob he might think, What is this guy doing running work if he can't handle this on his own?*

And finally, I convince myself not to call with, *Forget it, I'm just going to try and figure it out. I don't want anyone thinking I can't do my job.*

Can you see how self-perpetuating, unreasonable, and destructive this thinking is?

It's taken me many years of struggling through problems instead of swallowing my pride and picking up the phone to realize that there will never be a day when we know everything there is to know about our trades or our profession. There's simply too much to learn. So why not take advantage of the experience and expertise of those individuals you trust and respect?

Of course this equation works both ways: when you are respected and liked, those same individuals will bend over backwards to help you automatically.

Chapter 29

Give Yourself a Break

"I've been working in this industry for 30 years and I've never taken a vacation."

Sound familiar? When you've been around as many foreman and project managers as I have, you're sure to hear it a lot. These are individuals who claim they have never taken a break from work or a vacation. Supposedly they have spent their entire working lives moving directly from one job to the next, year after year, evidently because they are too "valuable" for any project to succeed without them.

Since I've known a number of these foremen my whole adult life, I know they are not being completely honest. Are they intentionally choosing to fudge the truth or have they truly forgotten?

My unfortunate conclusion about why these foremen would choose to "exaggerate" is that they feel it gets them something, perhaps furthers their status in the eyes of their peers. But you and I know that's the nice way of putting it. Truthfully, I think it can be summed up in one word: manipulation. Every time I heard them spouting this bit of hyperbole, I felt it was nothing more than an attempt to manipulate me to do what they wanted (usually to not take a vacation), but also to make me believe it was really my idea.

You're right. I can't be sure. But this is the way I felt nonetheless.

OBSESSED

Imagine what it would be like to take no time off for vacations with your family over a 40-year career! It makes me miserable just thinking about it. If you find yourself becoming so obsessed about the progress of your career that all your time and energy is focused on your job, I can promise you that one day you'll wake up full of regret about the course your personal life has or has not taken.

Sure, plenty of foremen talk about how they plan to take some time off, "as soon as the job is done." They'll even say something like, "Yeah, I won't be running work for a while; I need some time to decompress and let my brain unwind." Then, just before the project wraps up, their project manager begins priming them about an upcoming project. "It's yours to run," they say, "as soon as you can break free of this one."

You know what happens then. The idea of telling a project manager that you need some time off and that you'll be turning down an upcoming project suddenly doesn't look so good. In fact, I can't ever remember a time where someone I knew stood up for himself and his own needs over the wishes or needs of his company to say one simple word: "No."

We all have the desire to be important to our company and to the people we work for, but there are times when you have to say no for your own good.

Any company or project manager who respects and appreciates you and what you bring to the table on an ongoing basis will understand when you say you need a break. Unless they are profoundly shortsighted and incapable of empathy, they will find a way to encourage you to balance your personal and work life for everyone's benefit. The smart project manager knows that when a foreman's personal life is suffering or he has become mentally exhausted his performance at work will suffer as well.

Furthermore, those individuals who truly want what's best for your longevity and success will *insist* you take care of yourself to avoid the kind of burnout that leads to an early departure. It's common knowledge that when you work under extreme pressure and stress you need breaks to relax and recharge your batteries. Then you can come back refreshed and able to function at high capacity again. Look at it this way. If the President of the United States can take vacations, your company can probably get by for a week or two without you.

BALANCING ACT

This book is all about making a commitment to being the best you can be by doing everything you can to improve your skills as a leader. That's why there's no way to end it without a warning about the hazards of taking your ambition and desire to succeed too far.

In the best interest of your career, I strongly recommend that you put your health and welfare, along with the stability of your personal life, at the top of your list of priorities. I know how daunting a task it can be to perform this balancing act, especially when you're working so hard to make name for yourself on the job. Not only are you being pushed to the limits by others, but by your own drive. But focusing on work at the expense of home life means little time and energy for your loved ones.

Ultimately, when work takes a toll on your personal relationships, it becomes harder and harder to be your best at work. It is an unfortunate, but all too common, cycle of defeat.

Here is what I know after all these years of watching foremen (including myself) struggle to balance their two worlds: when one world is in shambles the other suffers as well. Of course if you're anything like me, you're probably saying, "That'll never happen to me. I won't let it happen. I'm different. I can be successful in both worlds." But even with the most sincere intentions this is easier said than done.

For that reason, I again offer you my two cents of advice:

Remain cognizant at all times that you do not drag what happens at work into your personal life and do not drag your personal life into work. I know, I know, easy to say, hard to do. But as long as you stay on top of managing each aspect of your life with intelligence, a realistic approach, and purpose, I believe it is possible to achieve success and happiness in both worlds.

THE WORKAHOLIC

There are always those who get an ego boost from being seen as the workaholic. You know, the person who gets it all done, who's always there. But in reality, this is someone who very likely has nowhere else to go. If you are like this, perhaps known as the foreman who works late, comes in on his day off, never takes a vacation, and "lives the job," you could be suffering from the illusion that your job will forever be secure. But this is never the case.

In truth, workaholics live a very lonely existence. While you are grinding out long hours attempting to make a good impression on those around you, those around you (including your bosses) are out living their lives. They aren't thinking about you and about how you choose to spend what should be your free time working instead.

Does it sound as if I am contradicting some of the things I said earlier when I tell you to take it easy and not push too hard? If so, let's revisit a few of the key items we talked about in previous chapters to clear up any confusion.

1. Planning properly allows you to complete tasks on *your* schedule so that very few surprises come your way.

2. Honing your organizational skills means peace of mind because you'll always know that your crewmembers can find what they need in a timely manner.

3. Practicing good communication leads to fewer misunderstandings and mistakes—for everyone.

4. Maintaining good crew morale leads to increased production.

5. When facing a new or difficult challenge, be willing to ask the people you trust and respect for help.

6. Managing your career decisions at a pace that is acceptable to you is the best approach.

When you learn and apply the strategies and habits
of truly successful foremen, your opportunities
will be limitless and you will become the foreman
others only aspire to be.

Conclusion

Final Thoughts on Success

Since the beginning of my career in the construction industry, I estimate that I have only worked with four or five really outstanding foremen. These were foremen who possessed the essential qualities of great leaders as heralded by their employers and peers. The others fall into two categories: the "mediocre majority" and the "temporary time bombs."

The question I pose to you is, *What kind of foreman are you going to be?*

I have discovered that individuals become foremen for many different reasons, and that holding the title doesn't mean being a great leader. In the ideal world, foremen would be chosen based on their skills in their trade; their ability to plan, organize, and problem solve; their ability to lead, direct, and motivate their crew; and their capacity to run each and every project efficiently and productively...all while being an exemplary representative of their company.

Unfortunately for most companies, few individuals possess all of these qualities.

I have spent over 20 years trying to figure out what it takes to be a great foreman. There have been times I was so frustrated I wanted to scream and throw in the towel, but there have also been times I was amazed when I watched a foreman overcome all odds to complete a project or face down challenges that would leave most of us begging for relief.

I have learned that there is no one approach to being a good foreman, but that the desire to be the best foreman you can be is what makes the difference between being great and being satisfied to just get by.

Construction Leadership Success uses the word "success" in the title for good reason. Success is important. We all want to reach our full potential and be regarded as successful professionals in whatever vocation we choose. Success defines us as individuals and fills us with pride and a sense of accomplishment.

But because the word "success" is subjective and because there really is no measuring tool for determining when we actually achieve it, I will share with you what success personally means to me. I have come to these conclusions honestly through decades of experience in the industry while working with many different people. This combination has shaped my perspective.

> » Success is fulfilling your commitments to your family, friends, employers, and coworkers at a level each one of them should be able to reasonably expect;

- » Success is being a team player; and
- » Success is helping others reach their potential in business *and* in life.

The funny thing about success is that you don't get to decide whether other people will agree with your assessment. They will make their own determinations based on their perception of your actions and the experiences you share together.

◻

If the information in this book helps you become the kind of foreman and leader you aspire to be, I will have done what I set out to do.

The choice is yours. The advice in this book coupled with your real world experiences will allow you to separate yourself from the crowd and ensure your services are always in demand. That means if you put everything you have into being a top-notch foreman, you can, and will, achieve success.

In conclusion, I advise you to be the kind of foreman for whom you would want to work, and to always treat your responsibilities as if it's your money on the line.

With these two approaches front and foremost whenever you face a difficult decision, you are sure to choose the correct one every single time.

Thanks, and good running.

Jason McCarty was born and raised in the Pacific Northwest and is a third-generation commercial/industrial electrician. His career in the construction industry began at the age of sixteen while working as a material handler and laborer throughout his high-school summers. After high school and two years of college he entered and completed a five-year electrical apprenticeship program in Portland, Oregon.

Over the span of his twenty-year career McCarty has worked on and/ or managed multiple construction projects, gaining the experience and knowledge outlined in **Construction Leadership Success**. The scope of these projects includes hospitals, schools, manufacturing facilities, industrial plants, corporate high rises, multi-resident high rises, retail establishments, and other facilities. The diverse nature of this work has provided McCarty with countless opportunities for studying the differing management styles that foremen employ to run and complete their projects.

McCarty's professional career as a journeyman electrician and foreman continues to shape his leadership and project management philosophies.

Made in United States
Orlando, FL
18 November 2024

54088510R00183